ADMEN AND EVE

The Bible in the Modern World, 48

Series Editors
J. Cheryl Exum, Jorunn Økland, Stephen D. Moore

Editorial Board
Alastair G. Hunter, Alison Jasper, Tat-siong Benny Liew,
Caroline Vander Stichele

Supported by the
Arts and Humanities Research Council

Arts & Humanities
Research Council

ADMEN AND EVE

THE BIBLE IN CONTEMPORARY ADVERTISING

Katie B. Edwards

SHEFFIELD PHOENIX PRESS

2012

Copyright © 2012 Sheffield Phoenix Press

Published by Sheffield Phoenix Press
Department of Biblical Studies, University of Sheffield
45 Victoria Street
Sheffield S3 7QB

www.sheffieldphoenix.com

A CIP catalogue record for this book
is available from the British Library

Typeset by Forthcoming Publications
Printed by Lightning Source

ISBN 978-1-907534-71-3
ISSN 1747-9630

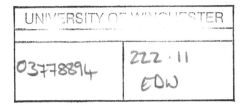

CONTENTS

PREFACE:
A GOOD RECEPTION?

This book came about from years spent reading glossy women's magazines and noticing a constant figure in the advertisements, Eve. Unmistakable, whether selling cars, clothes or ice cream, Eve and python and apple accessories remain regulars on the pages of the fashion monthlies.

I purposefully use Admen and Eve in the title because the images, although they are images that feature women and are targeted at women, are still created predominantly by male advertising executives in the advertising industry. The constant use of Eve imagery is not laziness on the part of those advertising executives either: Eve is an effective sales weapon. If these images proved unappealing to the target consumer then they would not be seen again. Market research is a multi-million pound business and every detail that can help advertisers to hone their target demographic more finely is utilized: age, employment status, disposable income, brand preferences, attitude to credit. They are all meticulously identified and then used in the battle for spending.

This book is a contribution to reception criticism of the Bible. Despite considerable attention to the reception of the Bible in film, art and music recently, advertising has continued to be a neglected area of study for biblical scholars.[1] Advertising, however, is a fertile ground for research

---

1. Influential contributions to research into the reception of the Bible include: J. Cheryl Exum, *Plotted, Shot and Painted: Cultural Representations of Biblical Women* (Sheffield: Sheffield Academic Press, 1996); Alice Bach, *Women, Seduction and Betrayal in Biblical Narrative* (Cambridge: Cambridge University Press, 1997); George Aichele and Richard Walsh (eds.), *Screening Scripture: Intertextual Connections between Scripture and Film* (Harrisburg, PA: Trinity Press International, 2002); Bruce Babington and Peter William Evans, *Biblical Epics: Sacred Narrative in the Hollywood Cinema* (Manchester: Manchester University Press, 1993); Alice Bach, 'With a Song in her Heart: Listening to Scholars Listening for Miriam', in *A Feminist Companion to Exodus to Deuteronomy* (ed. Athalya Brenner; Sheffield: Sheffield Academic Press, 1994), pp. 243-54; Bernard Brandon Scott, *Hollywood Dreams and Biblical Stories* (Minneapolis: Fortress Press, 1994); Martin O'Kane, *Painting the Text: The Artist as Biblical Interpreter* (Sheffield: Sheffield Phoenix Press, 2007); Yvonne Sherwood, *A Biblical Text and its Afterlives: The Survival*

into the cultural reception of biblical figures, and the biblical figure of Eve is the most frequently represented of them all. She is especially prominent in the postfeminist advertising (produced from 1990 onwards) that is treated in this book.

The reader may consider advertising to be a strange place to find research material for biblical studies, and yet popular magazines are a rich resource for cultural criticism of the Bible. Analysing contemporary advertising is similar to looking at a collage of images simultaneously reflecting and dictating the ideals, ideologies and iconography that inform the whole of Western culture. The iconography seen in fashion magazines is replicated and constantly updated in the most influential areas of popular culture, such as advertising, film, television, popular literature and album covers, all of which teach women and men how to see each other and themselves, how to treat each other and themselves and how to become their culturally dictated dream through the products they consume. Therefore, the fashion magazine, the popular film, the advertisement, together with the biblical text, become surprising sites for the exposure and subversion of the dominant cultural attitudes to gender roles.[2]

Despite the pervasive nature of advertising, I am aware from responses to many of the papers I have given at conferences that some academics are concerned that the analysis of the Bible in advertising detracts from the search for the 'original meaning' of the biblical text. For the purposes of this study I will follow Barthes's theory that the author is dead— literally, in this case. I do not believe that we can ever get to any 'origi- nal' or 'authorial' meaning in the text, that is, if authors are even aware of the full range of meanings their texts can create. We do not have and cannot retrieve authorial intention for the biblical text, but what we do

of *Jonah in Western Culture* (Cambridge: Cambridge University Press, 2000); J. Cheryl Exum and Ela Nutu (eds.), *Between the Text and the Canvas* (Sheffield: Sheffield Phoenix Press, 2007); Philip Culbertson and Elaine M. Wainwright (eds.), *The Bible in/and Popular Culture: A Creative Encounter* (Atlanta: Society of Biblical Literature, 2010); Beth Hawkins Benedix (ed.), *Subverting Scriptures: Critical Reflections on the Use of the Bible* (New York: Palgrave Macmillan, 2009).

2. A very common response to scholarly work on popular culture and in particular advertising is that it 'means nothing' or that it 'isn't meant to be taken seriously' (to take quotes from students of a Bible and Arts class at the University of Sheffield, dedicated to the analysis of the Bible in 'high' and popular culture). The notion that advertising is without ideology or political orientation seems fairly widespread and yet even a cursory glance at the images reveals definite gender roles in the 'story' of the image. Perhaps our way of viewing advertising images and the gender and racial ideologies implicit therein has become so naturalized that it is a difficult task to analyse those images.

have is the way the text functions right now, in front of eyes, and the meanings, messages and implicit social and cultural assumptions it is used to convey. That is the subject of this book, and the use of advertising to influence our desires, attitudes and behaviour is far from frivolous. Until very recently the enterprise of studying popular culture academically has been considered a somewhat trivial pursuit, not taken seriously by those in favour of more traditional academic subjects.[3] The notion that some subjects are more 'worthy' of study than others has come into sharp focus for those of us in the Arts and Humanities recently with the closure of university departments up and down the country. In particular, the threat of the closure of the Biblical Studies Department at the University of Sheffield in 2009 and other similar small departments at other universities brought out arguments about what constitutes 'worth' and 'value' in academia. The current political climate is based on the financial value of subjects: Will students be willing to get into considerable debt in order to study the subject? Will students/parents be prepared to pay out up to £9,000 in tuition fees to study the course? Does the subject allow the student to be a viable competitor in the job market? Does the subject earn its keep in terms of attracting not only students but also external funding? The argument that I often come across about the value of researching representation in popular culture as opposed to 'high' culture, however, is not based on economics, but usually on the basis that advertising, contemporary popular film etc. is not appropriate for academic study. I wonder, as academics are forced to consider the 'impact' of their research in order to achieve funding, how long it will be before biblical scholars begin to turn to contemporary popular culture as a means of demonstrating the social impact of their subject. Nevertheless, to create a distinction between subjects that are 'worth' studying and those that are not seems rather artificial and futile, and moreover it smacks of intellectual snobbery. What makes opera a more valid area of intellectual inquiry than hip-hop? Who says that the study of classical art is more worthwhile than the study of advertising? This book aims to show that, far from being frivolous and insignificant, popular culture is dense with biblical iconography exploited by the producers of popular culture as vehicles for implicit meanings, qualities and values to be communicated to the consumer.

---

3. See Andrew Ross, *No Respect: Intellectuals and Popular Culture* (New York: Routledge, 1989) for a far more comprehensive discussion of the relationship between intellectuals and popular culture.

ACKNOWLEDGMENTS

I have to share credit for this book with several people without whom my research could not have continued. This book developed from my PhD thesis, which was supported by an AHRC doctoral award from 2002 to 2004. AHRC sponsorship allowed me to attend conferences and give papers on my research, opportunities I may never otherwise have had and I am very grateful for them.

I would like to thank my Dad, Ross Edwards, for his tireless work in seeking out any images involving pythons and apples. I have never known anyone to complain so loudly about the content of women's magazines, but I deeply appreciate all the time and effort he continues to put into helping me with my research. Thank you, Dad. Thanks to my mum, Pam Edwards, for encouraging me to go on to study at University—you always know best, ma. I would like to thank my Dad, Ross Edwards, for his tireless work in seeking out any images involving pythons and apples. I have never known anyone to complain so loudly about the content of women's magazines, but I deeply appreciate all the time and effort he continues to put into helping me with my research. Thank you, Dad. A 'thank you' also goes to my other unofficial research assistant, Philippa Hardman, for sending on many images and articles over the years. Together, Ross and Philippa are the A-Team in the use of religious iconography in popular culture. My database would have been all the poorer without their help.

I would also like to thank Francesca Stavrakopoulou for her support and friendship, which I hold dear. SOTS simply would not be the same with you, Chessie. I am not sure this counts as a 'thank you' but I must show appreciation for my colleague, James Crossley, whose dulcet tones and inimitable phrasing cut through my writer's block like a rapier ('Oh, just get it done, Edwards').

Gratitude and appreciation must also go to David Clines and Ailsa Parkin at Sheffield Phoenix Press; thank you for all your kindness, patience and help.

That this book even exists is down to the patience and persistence of Cheryl Exum, without whom it is unlikely that I would even have discovered my interest in gender, sexuality and biblical imagery. It is through Professor Exum's Bible and the Arts class at the University of Sheffield, which I took as an undergraduate in 2000, that I started to collect the images I saw in magazines, and then started to look for them, and then started to document them in a database. It is because of Professor Exum's patience and support (and occasional glacial stare!) that I completed my PhD when life looked likely to abandon my thesis to the recesses of my laptop. I have Professor Exum to thank for a great many things, of which this book is only one—I dedicate it to her.

LIST OF FIGURES

Chapter 1

Chapter 2

Chapter 3

Chapter 4

INTRODUCTION:
SETTING THE SCENE

Why the hell should we care what a bunch of depressed, deluded, dead men said about a woman who never existed?

—Julie Burchill, 'All about Eve All Over Again'[1]

It is far more difficult to murder a phantom than a reality.

—Virginia Woolf, *A Room of One's Own*[2]

The burden of a tale that for thirty-five hundred years has taught women where they came from and what they're made of is not going to be shrugged off lightly in two decades.

—Naomi Wolf, *The Beauty Myth*[3]

Eve, in the style of all truly great cultural icons, embodies the *Zeitgeist* of the era: already Western society's premier *femme fatale*, Eve now functions as contemporary popular culture's pin-up girl for postfeminist female consumer power. And she is, it seems, everywhere these days, modelling crockery in the place of her traditional fig leaf for Versace, looking ravished for a Lolita Lempicka perfume campaign and, if we go to the cinema, we can even find her advertising a film in which she never

---

1. Julie Burchill, 'All about Eve All Over Again', *Guardian Unlimited* (Guardian Newspapers, 27 January 1999). Burchill's comment was made in reference to Pamela Norris's book, *The Story of Eve* (London: Papermac, 1999). It is clear that Burchill is not persuaded of the relevance of a book tracing the journey of Eve from biblical text to literature and art; however, Burchill seems to ignore the influence that Eve retains in contemporary culture, and appears not to recognize that people, both men and women who are very much alive, see images of Eve every day in advertising, music videos, film and popular literature. Perhaps we should not care what a bunch of dead men say about Eve 'who never existed' if those attitudes had no bearing on us now. But they do and those attitudes still echo in contemporary *femme fatale* imagery of Eve, who, while perhaps a mythical character, is still very much in evidence in the 'real' lives of all the girls, boys, women and men who partake of popular culture.

2. Virginia Woolf, *A Room of One's Own* (London: Flamingo, 1994).

3. Naomi Wolf, *The Beauty Myth: How Images of Beauty Are Used against Women* (London: Vintage, 1991), p. 94.

even appears.[4] While Pamela Norris has traced Eve's journey from biblical first lady to the archetypal sexual temptress we see in literature and fine art[5] and Theresa Sanders has catalogued the influence of the Adam and Eve story in twentieth-century popular culture,[6] what remains unexplored in biblical scholarship or otherwise is Eve's ubiquitous presence in contemporary advertising. This book seeks to make a contribution to this unexplored territory by analysing representations of Eve in examples of advertising from 1990 onwards, primarily because, as one of the major institutions of social representation in modern society, advertising is arguably the most influential cultural reflector and shaper of attitudes and beliefs about gender, sexuality and race.[7]

Because so much material is available on Eve in advertising, this book will deal almost exclusively with the analysis of white, heterosexual representations of Adam and Eve. The decision to limit the scope of the book in this way is not meant to place any greater value on white ethnicity or on heterosexuality but rather reflects contemporary advertisers' primary target: white, heterosexual female consumers. 'Heterosexual and white' is the 'norm' in Western popular culture and the vast majority of representations of Eve thus depict her as heterosexual and white. Sarah Projanksy criticizes postfeminist academic discourses for being 'limited [by their] overwhelming focus on white, heterosexual, middle-class women [and sometimes men]'.[8] This book belongs to the type of postfeminist academic discourse that Projansky criticizes for being 'limited', but in this case the limitation reflects the available data.

Contemporary images of Eve are definitional for women. Indeed, in contemporary Western culture the name 'Eve' has come to be synonymous with woman.[9] Eve's body, as it is portrayed in popular culture,

---

4. In Harry Ramis's 1999 film, *Bedazzled* (20th Century Fox), Elizabeth Hurley plays the character of the Devil in the storyline but represents Eve in the images that advertise the film on billboards and in magazines.

5. Norris, *The Story of Eve*.

6. Theresa Sanders, *Approaching Eden: Adam and Eve in Popular Culture* (London: Rowman & Littlefield, 2009).

7. Since I call my work, and myself, feminist then it is clear that my study takes a particular political position. Feminism, the representation of women in popular culture and the representation of women in the most influential literature in Western culture have an effect on my life and on those around me, so I read for my own interests. Every reader does to an extent but some are more self-conscious about it than others.

8. Sarah Projansky, *Watching Rape: Film and Television in Postfeminist Culture* (New York: New York University Press, 2001), p. 68.

9. The name 'Eve' is often given to products that target an exclusively female consumer. See, for example, Eve cigarettes (introduced to the market in 1971) and the

represents the collective bodies of women so that her image in advertising is a reflection of how women are viewed and how they should view themselves, as illustrated in Chapter 3. The archetypal image of the sexual temptress who proffers fruit to a bewildered-looking male and the pseudo-sinister sexual appeal of the woman/snake conflation are used in contemporary culture as evidence of women's potent sexual allure. The popular ideology of postfeminist advertising suggests that the ability to attract the opposite sex allows women to obtain sexual power and, the advertisers would have us believe, financial independence through their devastating effect on men.

What's Postfeminism Got to Do with It?

Since the 1960s and '70s, when the media became increasingly identified as the 'machinery of representation'[10] in modern society and 'an institution of ideological control with the power to construct meaning about the world and represent it to the public in many different and conflicting ways',[11] feminists began to recognize the importance of popular cultural representations of women in influencing and reflecting societal attitudes to women. The media was criticized by feminist scholars for its representations of women, which seemed wholly defined by male priorities. Scholars of advertising found that women were consistently objectified and subjugated in advertisements,[12] and, with the massive social change brought about by second-wave feminism, advertising began to incorporate some of the more profitable aspects of feminism into its images. Before the advent of second-wave feminism, male advertising executives

recent launch of Carlsberg's Eve lower-calorie and alcohol content drink. According to Carlsberg's product press kit, 'The name is used internationally—Eve is a synonym for women and femininity… Eve is for the cosmopolitan and sophisticated woman aged 25–35 years old' (http://www.carlsberggroup.com/media/PressKits/brands/Pages/EvePressKit.aspx [accessed 20 December 2010]).

    10. Stuart Hall, 'Media Power and Class Power', in J. Curran *et al.* (eds.), *Bending Reality: The State of the Media* (London: Pluto Press, 1986), pp. 5-14 (9).

    11. Vicki Coppock, Deena Haydon and Ingrid Richter, *The Illusions of Post-Feminism: New Women, Old Myths* (London: Taylor & Francis, 1995), p. 107.

    12. See Erving Goffman's trailblazing study of gender representation in advertising, *Gender Advertisements* (London: Macmillan, 1979), Judith Williamson's seminal work on encoded social messages in advertising, *Decoding Advertisements: Ideology and Meaning in Advertising* (London: Marion Boyers Publishers, 2000), first published in 1978, and Trevor Millum's pioneering research on the representation of females in women's magazines of the 1970s, *Images of Woman: Advertising in Women's Magazines* (London: Chatto & Windus, 1975).

objectified women in visual culture for a male consumer. In contemporary postfeminist advertising, the woman frequently objectifies herself for own agenda and financial gain. A huge number of female celebrities from Katie Price to Kate Moss have posed as Eve to advance or maintain their status as sexy, edgy models or actresses. Postfeminist advertising does not so much sell and objectify women per se but has women objectifying and selling *themselves*.[13]

In postfeminist popular culture, female sexuality represents female power and is the avenue through which women can achieve social ambitions and power in gender relations. In the images analysed in this book, it would seem that some of the aims of feminism are realized: women are in control of their sexuality, so long dominated by men; they enjoy financial autonomy and, far from achieving social equality with men, thanks to the traditional feminine wiles of male manipulation through sex appeal, women have a way to dominate, subdue and control men. Much of the contemporary advertising treated for the purposes of this study appropriates and transforms feminist politics into one handily marketable commodity. The advertisements are selling the concept of female empowerment and sexual autonomy through images of Eve, a postfeminist social construction of femininity.

The term 'postfeminist' is used throughout the book to describe the ideology in which the advertisements are anchored. Postfeminism has

---

13.   Carol J. Adams, *The Pornography of Meat* (London: Continuum, 2003); Jennifer Baumgardner and Amy Richards, *ManifestA: Feminism, the Future and Young Women* (New York: Farrar, Straus & Giroux, 2000); Ann Brooks, *Postfeminisms: Feminism, Cultural Theory, and Cultural Forms* (London: Routledge, 1997); Delilah Campbell, 'This Article Degrades Advertisements', *Trouble and Strife* 35 (1997), pp. 30-39; Sarah Ciriello, 'Commodification of Women: Morning, Noon and Night', in Emilie Buchwald, Pamela R. Fletcher and Martha Roth (eds.), *Transforming a Rape Culture* (Minneapolis: Milkweed Editions, 1993), pp. 265-81; Coppock, Haydon and Richter, *The Illusions of Post Feminism*; Tab Friend, 'The Rise of "Do Me" Feminism', *Esquire* (February 1994), pp. 48-56; Stacy Gillis and Rebecca Munford, *Feminism and Popular Culture: Explorations in Postfeminism* (London: I.B. Tauris, 2007); Robert Goldman, Deborah Heath and Sharon L. Smith, 'Commodity Feminism', *Critical Studies in Mass Communication* 8 (1991), pp. 333-51; Robert Goldman, *Reading Ads Socially* (London: Routledge, 1992); Leslie Heywood and Jennifer Drake, 'Introduction', in Leslie Heywood and Jennifer Drake (eds.), *Third Wave Agenda: Being Feminist, Doing Feminism* (Minneapolis: University of Minnesota Press, 2003), pp. 1-24; Ariel Levy, *Female Chauvinist Pigs: Women and the Rise of Raunch Culture* (New York: Free Press, 2005); A. Rochelle Mabry, 'About a Girl: Female Subjectivity and Sexuality in Contemporary "Chick" Lit Culture', in Suzanne Ferris and Malory Young (eds.), *Chick Lit: The New Woman's Fiction* (London: Routledge, 2005), pp. 191-207; Patricia S. Mann, *Micro-Politics: Agency in a Postfeminist Era* (Minneapolis: University of Minnesota Press, 1994).

become a buzzword for describing popular discourse since second-wave feminism, and has become a slippery term in academia, due to the distinct lack of consensus as to what the term actually means.[14] The present book does not attempt to contribute to a debate about the 'true meaning' of postfeminism, since postfeminism, like feminism, is an umbrella term that encompasses diverse ideologies that share a concern with the representation and attitudes of, and to, women who now have the rights and (albeit still limited) economic autonomy afforded to them since second-wavefeminism became mainstream in contemporary culture.[15]

Some of the many forms postfeminism can take are outlined by Sarah Projansky in her groundbreaking work, *Watching Rape*.[16]

Linear Postfeminism: describes discourses that suggest that postfeminism has supplanted feminism and therefore feminism no longer exists.

Backlash Postfeminism: defines discourses that do not declare feminism over but retaliate against feminism, in what Projanksy describes as 'antifeminist feminist postfeminism'. Backlash postfeminism offers a 'new' feminism as an improvement on the 'old' flawed feminism.

New Traditionalist Postfeminism: harks back to prefeminist gender ideals and roles that were supposedly destroyed by the advent of feminism. New Traditionalist Postfeminism and Backlash Postfeminism are very closely linked since they both hold feminism in a particularly negative light and New Traditionalist Postfeminism is, in itself, a form of backlash against the social changes that feminism brought about.

14. See Diane Negra's work on the problems of postfeminism in academia, *What a Girl Wants? Fantasizing the Reclamation of Self in Postfeminism* (London: Routledge, 2009), and also the *Interrogating Postfeminism: Gender and the Politics of Contemporary Culture* conference (April 2004), co-organized by Negra, Yvonne Tasker and Judith Ashby, which addressed the problematic nature of the term 'postfeminism' for scholars of popular culture. As the conference's Call for Papers explains, 'Some of the most vibrant recent work in media studies research explores the increasing proliferation of popular cultural texts which seek to construct and address women as consumers. The notion of "post-feminism" has, implicitly and explicitly, been a staple feature of this proliferation, yet there still exists little consensus or clarity about what it really means and what its relationship with feminist scholarship should be. Both within academic and mainstream cultural forums, current definitions of post-feminism are multiple, contentious and often contradictory: for some, post-feminism constitutes a playful and empowering new phase in feminism's relationship to popular culture; for others, it is another means through which feminist cultural politics may be diluted and misappropriated by the mainstream media.' Papers from the conference were published in the edited volume, Yvonne Tasker and Diane Negra (eds.), *Interrogating Postfeminism: Gender and the Politics of Popular Culture* (London: Duke University Press, 2007).

15. Chapter 2 will discuss the illusory female financial equality assumed in postfeminist advertising.

16. Projansky, *Watching Rape*, pp. 67-68.

Equality and Choice Postfeminism: This form of postfeminism credits feminism with the achievement of gender equality and having given women
'choice'.[17] This type of postfeminism sees feminism in a relatively positive
light; however, it does suggest that, if women have achieved equity and
choice, then feminism is no longer necessary.

(Hetero)sex Positive Postfeminism: In (Hetero)sex Positive Postfeminist
discourse feminism is defined as being inherently antisex. This type of postfeminism is then offered as a more contemporary, more positive, alternative to
the other types of feminism. Again, this form of postfeminism does not reject
feminism completely, since it relies on aspects of feminism that promise
women's independence. In other words, it both rejects feminism on the
grounds that it is antisex and embraces it because of its focus on individuality
and independence. In most postfeminist discourse of this type, men are background figures, featuring only as villains, role models or objects of desire.[18]

It is important to recognize the many forms that postfeminism can
take, even though not all the forms of postfeminism delineated by
Projansky are represented in the material investigated in this book.
Throughout this study I use the generic term 'postfeminism' to describe
the ideologies and attitudes encoded in contemporary Eve advertisements, namely, the ideologies of Equality and Choice and (Hetero)sex
Positive Postfeminisms. These ideologies portray female sexuality as
irresistible to the rather docile modern man and portray the modern
woman as knowing how to make her body work in her favour. The sexually attractive woman can have it all: money, power in gender relations
and social superiority among her peers. This study exposes the commercial, social and cultural factors that make this postfeminist capitalist
image of Eve/woman so appealing to producers of popular culture and
consumers alike.

The Aims of this Book

Advertisers constantly recycle images of Eve because she is a cultural
icon, easily recognizable to the target consumer, allowing producers of
popular culture to exploit the cultural mythology that surrounds her and
communicate implicit gender codes to the consumer. In magazine print

17.   Despite the fact that postfeminist advertisements, and the ones analysed in this
book, tend to reflect Equality and Choice and (Hetero)sex positive postfeminisms, it
seems that women 'choose' to represent themselves only in the same ways that men
have represented them in the past. Has this new-found ability to 'choose' made any
difference to women in that case?
18.   A characteristic of the contemporary Adam and Eve advertisements analysed in
this book.

advertising, when brands have less than a second between page turns to make an impact on the consumer, an image is worth a thousand words and Eve proves to be excellent value. The combination of a woman, an apple and/a snake is instantly recognized as a symbol of temptation and desirable female sexuality by consumers. In popular culture, Eve becomes the signifier for female sexual temptation as a route to achieving social power.

This book is concerned with the predominant stereotype of the sexual female in postfeminist advertising. It enquires into the power dynamics that inform the stereotype. The following chapters will investigate from various angles how the power advertising sells to women is problematic. The empowered New Woman of postfeminist consumer cultures uses her sexuality as a means of gaining power and influence in society. Consequently, postfeminist advertising portrays the male in the images as a victim of the charms of the female and often pictures him as docile, passive or submissive, illustrating the power of female sexuality to strip the male of his traditional role of dominance. Postfeminist advertising simplifies the sexual dynamics between the male and female to a straightforward transaction of power from the male to the female: the female is empowered through the male's desire for her and the male is disempowered by that same desire. The woman's sexual desire, however, is not part of the transaction. In *Gender and the Media* Rosalind Gill argues that 'one of the major shifts in advertising over the last decade or so has been the shift from the portrayal of women as sex objects to the portrayal of women as active and desiring sexual subjects'[19] and yet in Eve advertisements where she is pictured with Adam, she rarely shows desire for him. She may well show desire for the product being sold (if the product is even featured in the advertisement), usually fashion accessories, cosmetics or chocolate, which, the advertisement suggests, can offer her confidence, empowerment and satisfaction, but in the hundreds of Eve advertisements I have collected over ten years of research it is noticeable that Eve does not return Adam's desire for her. The focus is on her ability to attract the gaze and maintain that attraction through the consumption of (often luxury) cosmetics and clothing.[20]

19. Rosalind Gill, *Gender and the Media* (Cambridge, MA: Polity Press, 2007), p. 89.
20. This pattern seems to be part of a wider popular cultural trend to represent women as sexy and sexually appealing but not sexually active. Successful postfeminist heroines must simultaneously attract *and* distance themselves from male sexual attention because should they return the desire and become sexually involved then they lose their worth as an object of desire. This pattern is most clearly exemplified in Chanel's 2011 advertisement for the *Coco Mademoiselle* fragrance starring the actress Keira

The influence of the cultural emblems found in Genesis 2–3 on contemporary visual culture is not, as Athalya Brenner writes, 'on the decline but is still wide-spread';[21] rather, the cultural emblems found in Genesis 2–3 are currently enjoying a resurgence. New advertisements featuring Adam and Eve, and, more popularly, Eve, with her trusty apple and python, are being created and published all the time. These advertisements are everywhere in popular culture. We are bombarded with stereotypes of Eve as temptress and Adam as dupe, so that most contemporary readers' interpretations of the biblical text will quite likely be influenced by these popular cultural representations, even if only at a subliminal level and even if these readers are familiar with the biblical text.[22]

What I am concerned with in this book is: What aspects of the biblical text are exaggerated in the advertising images and why? What aspects of the text are downplayed or even ignored and why? This study, in reading the biblical text in conjunction with its popular cultural interpretations, acknowledges the influence of the text in contemporary Western society rather than its authority. The aim of the book is not to reclaim or redeem the text, nor to reclaim or redeem Eve, rather, the aim of the book is to

---

Knightley. In the advertisement Knightley, dressed in nude coloured biker gear with 'It's a Man's, Man's, Man's World' as the backing track, drives her motorbike to a photoshoot where she gradually seduces the photographer, getting him to undress her and photograph her naked before lying back on the bed as if inviting him to kiss her. When the photographer does attempt a kiss, Knightley blocks his mouth with her hand and asks him to lock the door. We see the door lock and the photographer, shirt unbuttoned, turn back to the bed to find Knightley gone, the room empty but the French windows open with the curtains billowing in the breeze. The photographer runs to the window and looks out to find a fully dressed Knightley back on her motorbike ready to drive away. As the photographer looks on, Knightley tucks a miniature bottle of Coco Mademoiselle into the breast of her zip-up jacket and drives off with a wry smile. The Chanel advertisement clearly communicates that successful, enviable women must attract male sexual desire but not act on it. It is female sexual self-objectification rather than any authentic female sexuality that is valued in postfeminist popular culture. See Chapter 3 for a further discussion of the simultaneous 'attract and distance' techniques successful postfeminist celebrities employ in self-promotional images. View the advertisement at http://fashion.telegraph.co.uk/videos/TMG8396363/Keira-Knightleys-Chanel-Coco-Mademoiselle-advert.html (accessed 16 July 2012).

21.   Athalya Brenner, 'Introduction', in Athalya Brenner (ed.), *A Feminist Companion to Genesis* (Sheffield: Sheffield Academic Press, 1997), p. 13.

22.   Cf. J. Cheryl Exum's comments about cultural appropriations of female biblical characters because: 'What many people know or think they know about the Bible often comes more from familiar representations of biblical texts and themes in the popular culture than from study of the ancient text itself' (*Plotted, Shot and Painted: Cultural Representations of Biblical Women* [Sheffield: Sheffield Academic Press, 1996]), pp. 8-9.

consider how Eve's character functions in the temptation story and in popular culture. How is she represented in the text? What themes and motifs are used in conjunction with Eve and what do they imply about her? Are the themes emphasized in popular culture already inscribed in the text? Does the text lend itself to the prevalent popular cultural readings of Genesis 2–3, to the representations of Eve? What in the text gives rise to these ideas? What challenges them? Such are the questions that I want to ask of the biblical text, and the advertising images in which Eve is depicted.

My aim is not to argue for a 'true' or objective reading of Genesis 2–3—or indeed, to engage in an in-depth study of a text about which so much scholarly literature already exists—but rather to show how the cultural tradition of viewing Eve as a sexual seductress, whose sexuality is both her power to influence men and her reason for subordination, has its roots in Genesis 2–3. In contrast to popular cultural portrayals of Eve, some feminist biblical scholars have sought to reclaim, redeem, re-establish or deconstruct Genesis 2–3 for womanly readers.[23] Striving to recover Eve from her cultural status as temptress, feminist critics have scoured the narrative for positive interpretations of the Bible's first woman and her role in the 'fall' of humanity.[24] Whereas popular culture has emphasized female sexuality and exaggerated the role of the sexual power dynamics between Adam and Eve, in contrast, some second-wave feminist biblical scholars have refuted any interpretation of Genesis 2–3 that emphasizes sex or sexual relations,[25] while others have suggested that the text, arguably the most influential cultural document for gender relations in Western society, is beyond redemption and attempts to reclaim the text from patriarchy are futile.[26] This book does not intend to try to

23. See Phyllis Trible, *God and the Rhetoric of Sexuality* (Philadelphia: Fortress Press, 1978), pp. 72-143; Reuven Kimelman, 'The Seduction of Eve and the Exegetical Politics of Gender', *Biblical Interpretation* 4 (1996), pp. 1-39; Mieke Bal, *Lethal Love: Feminist Literary Readings of Biblical Love Stories* (Bloomington: Indiana University Press, 1987); Helen Schungel-Straumann, 'On the Creation of Man and Woman in Genesis 1–3: The History and Reception of the Texts Reconsidered', in Brenner (ed.), *A Feminist Companion to Genesis*, pp. 53-76.

24. For instance, Trible, *God and the Rhetoric of Sexuality*, and Kimelman, 'The Seduction of Eve and the Exegetical Politics of Gender'.

25. Ilana Pardes, *Countertraditions in the Bible* (Cambridge, MA: Harvard University Press, 1992) and Carey Ellen Walsh, *Exquisite Desire: Religion, the Erotic and the Song of Songs* (Minneapolis: Fortress Press, 2000).

26. Pamela Milne, 'The Patriarchal Stamp of Scripture: The Implications of Structuralist Analyses for Feminist Hermeneutics', in Brenner (ed.), *A Feminist Companion to Genesis*, pp. 146-72.

discredit feminist readings of Genesis 2–3 that seek to provide positive re-readings of the biblical material. Such an approach is understandable and even admirable; however, this study does critique feminist approaches that have chosen to side-step problematic areas of the text in favour of more 'positive' aspects that more conveniently fulfil the needs of their reading agendas. Such interpretations are entirely unhelpful in trying to understand the story's function and influence in contemporary culture. Interpretations, I argue, are not created independently of the text, but rather are created in a mutual relationship of reader and text, where, while the reader's 'extra-text'[27] may affect their interpretation of the text to a certain extent, the text limits or controls the semantic range for the reader.[28]

To illustrate this point, Chapter 1, 'Genesis 2–3: The Creation of an Icon', describes how the biblical text contains encoded gender messages, which need to be decoded and exposed to understand the influence of the biblical text on contemporary popular cultural gender politics. In this chapter, I read the biblical text against contemporary advertising images to argue that, when advertisers make the sexual temptation of Adam by Eve the theme of the story, they are picking up on a theme implicit in the biblical text even though they may exaggerate its importance. In Chapter 2, 'The Never-changing Face of Eve: Representations of Eve in Nineteenth Century Fin-de-Siècle Art and Twentieth Century Fin-de-Siècle Advertising', I read examples of popular cultural Eve images against her nineteenth century artistic representations to show that not only has the image itself remained unchanged throughout massive political, social, cultural and economic change but also the meanings associated with the image have remained constant too. What has changed is the way the image functions in contemporary society: postfeminist advertising promotes a kind of pseudo-liberation for female consumers; it suggests that because women objectify themselves where previously they were objectified, then women are freed from centuries of male control. In doing so, however, advertising posits the female as simultaneously subject and object, and thus this 'liberation', as suggested above, is only half-hearted. Whereas nineteenth century works of art, in response to first-wave feminism, condemn the New Woman as a threat to social order, postfeminism dismisses feminism altogether in favour of female empowerment through the exploitation of women's own sexuality as a commodity.

27. I use the term 'extra-text' here to describe all the 'baggage' that a reader brings to a text: taking for granted that every experience, book, film, etc. to which a reader is exposed influences their reading of a text.
28. Milne, 'The Patriarchal Stamp of Scripture', p. 171.

Chapter 3, 'Bad Girls Sell Well: The Commodification of Eve in Postfeminist Consumerism', examines this phenomenon of postfeminist consumerism. Advertisers use images of Eve as temptress in order to sell to women the ideal of female heterosexual sexuality as a means to obtain power. This chapter argues that the power offered by postfeminist advertising is both problematic and, because of the primary focus on the individual and her choice, divisive for women. Eve advertisements are part of a wider consumer trend to encourage women to concentrate on personal consumer choice rather than collectively campaigning to bring about social change to obtain equal pay or to redress the imbalance in childcare—the issues that genuinely affect women's ability to achieve social status and equality.

The fourth and final chapter of the book, 'Forbidden Fruit Always Tastes the Sweetest: Eve Imagery in the Twilight and Desperate Housewives Franchises' focuses on promotional images from the TV series *Desperate Housewives* (2004–12) and the film *Twilight* (2008), which use forbidden fruit symbolism to market concepts of temptation, desire and, I argue, postfeminist consumer choice to a predominantly female audience.

This book will illustrate how images of Eve in postfeminist advertising are used to promote an ideology that focuses on female sexuality and the use of traditional feminine wiles as a means for women to obtain power in a society that, contradictorily, is assumed to have already achieved gender equality. Images of Eve, despite their appearance of conventional gender-role subversion, in fact reinscribe traditional roles for men and women, and reflect the gender codes embedded in the biblical text. Nevertheless, this book also acknowledges that these images are popular and pleasurable for many women. It would be unfair to dismiss that pleasure as 'wrong' or inappropriate (and I am a huge fan of popular culture myself) because the benefits being sold are problematic for those buying in to them. Instead, I hope to investigate what it is that makes these images so pleasurable for consumers and the reasons for Eve's cultural tenacity. Let us begin with the creation of a cultural icon.

1

Genesis 2–3:
The Creation of an Icon

With a taste of your lips,
I'm on a ride,
You're toxic,
I'm slipping under,
With a taste of a poison paradise,
I'm addicted to you,
Don't you know that you're toxic?
And I love what you do,
But you know that you're toxic.

—Britney Spears, *Toxic*[1]

Heterosexual men, on beholding an attractive female body, insistently divide it into edible parts; for centuries, the female beloved has been subjected to a scrutiny as critical as that of a greengrocer examining the latest crop of apples before deciding whether to buy… It's a striking feature of men's imagery of woman-as-food that it's frequently vegetarian, transforming the object of desire into luscious fruit-like figs and cherries. Men are also happy to think of their female lovers as tender birds of prey but not as creatures with hooves, teeth and a predatory appetite of their own. Whoever heard of a fig—or indeed an oyster—biting back?

—Joan Smith, *Hungry for You*[2]

1.   Although Spears is singing about a man's irresistible sexual attraction being 'toxic' here, in the promotional video she is the one portrayed as the *femme fatale*. She is depicted in a variety of 'temptress' scenarios, where, in various guises (flight attendant, superhero in black catsuit and naked covered in diamonds), she kisses various rather ordinary looking men, ultimately feeding poison to the final 'toxic' male in the line. Thus, while the lyrics of the song suggest that a male's kiss is intoxicating, it is a different case in the video, which subscribes to the rather fashionable postfeminist attitude that a sexually attractive woman exercises, or is capable of exercising, enormous power over the male. In the video it is her kiss that is the toxic 'poison paradise' and not the man's. The director of the video, Joseph Kahn, said of Spears, 'That's part of her brilliance… She totally understands that she's naughty and nice, that she's the *girl next door* gone bad who is constantly titillating you. She's not like most artists who flaunt their pure sexuality.' Britney Spears, *Toxic* (BMG, 2004).
2.   Joan Smith, *Hungry for You* (London: Vintage, 1997), p. 85.

He needed women as mother Figures and mistresses and at the same time
bitterly resented their power over him.
—Patrick Bade, *Femme fatale*[3]

It is well documented that Eve has been the victim of centuries of bad
press by interpreters.[4] In art and literature she has been portrayed as the
ultimate temptress, the biblical bad girl whose predatory sexuality lured
Adam into disobedience and out of Eden; a seductress whose powers of
attraction were so potent that she caused the fall not only of Adam, but
of the whole of humanity. Her tarnished reputation has been turned on
its head in modern-day advertisements, however.

Figure 1.0. *Still of TV advertisement for POM Wonderful Juice, 2010*[5]

3. Patrick Bade, *Femme Fatale: Images of Evil and Fascinating Women* (New York:
Mayflower Books, 1979), p. 24.
4. See Norris, *The Story of Eve*, for a comprehensive guide to the many religious and
literary interpretations of Eve as temptress. See also Elizabeth K. Menon, *Evil by Design:
The Creation and Marketing of the Femme Fatale* (Urbana: University of Illinois Press,
2006), for analysis of *femme fatale* Eve imagery in French popular sources from 1885–
1910, and Theresa Sanders for a guide to Eve's presence in pre-1950's film and radio.
5. This campaign for the pomegranate juice POM Wonderful featured three advertisements all shown on prime-time TV. In addition to Eve, two further advertisements,
one featuring Aphrodite and the other a Persian Warrior, were shown. In the Eve
advert, Eve is played by Sonja Kinski, the daughter of Natasha Kinski, the actress whose
naked pose with a python photographed by Richard Avedon in 1981 was marketed as a
poster and is now an iconic image. The Avedon/Kinski image has received renewed
attention in recent years thanks to the online parodies of the 2006 film *Snakes on a
Plane*, starring Samuel L. Jackson, which include 'Snakes on a Dame', a collection of
images of naked models and actresses with snakes and 'Snakes on a Playmate', Playboy's
attempt to cash in on the trend (content available to fee-paying Playboy Club members
only). The casting of Sonja Kinski for the part of Eve is no coincidence: the link

As Figure 1.0 illustrates, contemporary advertising perpetuates the age-old reading of Eve as the embodiment of desirable sin and emphasizes the sexual nature of Eve's transgression. In this TV advertisement for POM Wonderful, a python writhes over Eve while a voice-over intones: 'Some scholars believe it wasn't an apple, but a ruby-red, antioxidant-rich pomegranate, with which Eve tempted Adam. And only POM Wonderful has the juice of four whole pomegranates and is backed by modern science. Powerful then. POM Wonderful now.' Consumers, used to seeing Eve with a red apple to signify the forbidden fruit, are informed that here Eve has been tempted by new pomegranate juice brand POM Wonderful. In many images, as in the one above, Adam is not even present; we, the viewer, are supposed to take his place. These images are aimed at a female consumer, who is expected to adopt the position of male to assess herself. John Berger's comment about painting is applicable here:

> Men *act* and *women appear*. Men look at women. Women watch themselves being looked at. This determines not only most relations between men and women but also the relation of women to themselves. The surveyor of woman in herself is male: the surveyed female. Thus she turns herself into an object—and most particularly an object of vision: a sight.[6]

In contemporary Eve imagery, in contrast to the literary and artistic representations of Eve in the past, female self-objectification has become the basic tenet of postfeminist popular culture. Advertising that targets young women promotes a form of power that is centred around female sexuality, its manipulation and its objectification for the benefit of women, who will, advertising suggests, gain social status and power in gender relations from attracting the gaze. As the examples set out in the following chapters show, by postfeminist advertising standards, a successful powerful woman must attract both the female and the male gazes: the male through sexual desire and the female through envious desire—the desire to be like her. This is in contrast to more traditional images of Eve, which have denounced her for being a *femme fatale* and a temptress. Postfeminist popular culture attempts to turn what was once viewed as a negative (images of Eve as temptress) into a positive message of self-empowerment for young women.

between Sonja Kinski's Eve and her mother's famous pose not only creates extra press attention around the advertisement but also ensures that the concepts of cultural and mythical icons and female sexuality are well cemented in the minds of the viewers.

6.   John Berger, *Ways of Seeing* (London: Penguin Books, 1977), p. 47 (emphasis original).

Figure 1.1. *Print Advertisement for Original Sin Cider, 2008*

Figure 1.1, an advertisement for Original Sin cider, is an example of how advertising has picked up on Adam's minor role in the transgression scene—here, he is entirely absent. In contrast to the active and engaged Eve, who tempts Adam and the consumer with her often naked body and proffered apple (it is almost always an apple in advertising, or a bottle shaped to resemble an apple), Adam, on the occasions when he is included in the image, is usually depicted in a state of licensed withdrawal (Fig. 1.2). 'Licensed withdrawal', a term coined by sociologist Erving Goffman in *Gender Advertisements*, his groundbreaking analysis of the advertising of the 1970s, refers to the technique used by advertisers to distance a character from the action in an advertisement, to remove

them from responsibility for the action by having them look away from
both the viewer and the active figure in the image.[7] Licensed withdrawal
allows advertisers to make one person appear child-like, thereby giving
the impression that another character in the advertisement has the
higher social status and greater responsibility for any action taking place.

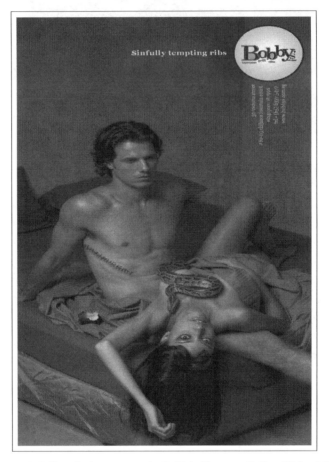

Figure 1.2. *Billboard advertisement for Bobby's Taproom Grill and Ribs, 2008*[8]

7. Goffman, *Gender Advertisements*, pp. 57-83.
8. Unusually for Eve advertisements, the billboard advertisement for Bobby's
Taproom Grill and Ribs in Singapore (Fig. 1.2) promotes a restaurant/bar for a mainly
male clientele. As we will see later in Chapter 3, often the Eve images directed to men
and those directed to women are very similar.

Figure 1.3. *Print advertisement for Leeds Victoria Quarter, 2004*

In the case of Adam and Eve, it is Eve who is given the lion's share of the blame for any temptation taking place. But unlike women in traditional advertisements, who are usually shown in a state of licensed withdrawal,[9] Eve is simultaneously given the higher social status and responsibility in the transgression episode. If Adam is engaged in the action in the picture, he will be looking at Eve, whom he appears to find irresistible, but Eve is always pictured as unaware of him, and, without fail, stares back at the viewer, returning our gaze (Fig. 1.3). This situation recalls Adam's lack of narrative presence in the text, where he plays a small role in the transgression. A passive man and an active woman— this is what advertisers hope that female consumers will find appealing about images of Eve. These advertisements are designed to appeal to postfeminist female consumers who are attracted to images of apparently

    9. See Anthony J. Cortese, *Provocateur: Images of Women and Minorities in Advertising* (Lanham: Rowman & Littlefield, 1999), pp. 33-34; Goffman, *Gender Advertisements*, pp. 57-83.

autonomous female sexuality and of female sexuality as empowerment, sexuality not just unfettered by male domination but sexuality that dominates males. Women are offered the opportunity to turn the tables on traditional gender dynamics and buy the power to influence men through the consumption of material goods.

In spite of the analyses of biblical scholars such as Trible[10] and Kimelman,[11] among others who have attempted egalitarian readings of the text, Genesis 2–3 remains popular with advertisers because it offers the opportunity to explore and exploit contemporary heterosexual gender roles and the distribution of power in sexual relations. Can we dismiss centuries upon centuries of interpretation of Eve as a temptress responsible for the 'fall' of humanity by introducing sin and evil into the world as so much mis-reading? The biblical scholar Schungel-Straumann would have us do so.[12] She argues that the woman and man are equal in the biblical text in spite of the patriarchal context in which the story was created and that 'women have to reclaim this gender equality of image and power from traditional and historical interpretations through a return to the text'.[13] She observes:

> Why could these narratives be used to make women responsible for human-kind's sin and evil? There were two major stages leading to this: the first was the interpreting of the Fall in such a way that the woman's role in it was seen to be greater then the man's. The second was the generalization; *one* woman equals *all* women.[14]

10.   Trible, 'A Love Story Gone Awry', in *God and the Rhetoric of Sexuality*, pp. 72-143.

11.   Kimelman, 'The Seduction of Eve and the Exegetical Politics of Gender'.

12.   Schungel-Straumann, 'On the Creation of Man and Woman in Genesis 1–3'.

13.   This quote is taken from Athalya Brenner's summary of Schungel-Straumann's conclusion in the Introduction to *A Feminist Companion to Genesis*, p. 15. Schungel-Straumann's suggestion that readers can 'reclaim' gender equality through a return to the text seems to ignore the fact that the responsibility for interpretation does not lie with the reader alone. Meaning is created in the interaction between the text and the reader; while it is certainly possible for multiple interpretations to arise from one text, it is also likely that a text will give rise to very similar interpretations since the semantic field of the text is relatively limited, as Pamela Milne comments: 'Placing the locus of meaning so completely within the reading subject leads me to ask whether it matters if a reader is reading the Bible or Ku Klux Klan literature. If the text does not limit or control the semantic range in any way, then surely we should not worry about such things as hate literature since only those readers who are already committed to anti-Semitism, racism, sexism or anti-feminism will read hate literature as hate literature. I do not think any text, biblical or not, contains "real meaning" but rather that texts put constraints on the range within which meanings are constructed.' Milne, 'The Patriarchal Stamp of Scripture', pp. 170-71.

14.   Schungel-Straumann, 'On the Creation of Man and Woman in Genesis 1–3', p. 55.

On the contrary, one could argue that traditional interpretations have been perpetuated in Western culture because the woman's role in the transgression episode *was* greater than the man's and Eve *does* represent womankind in the text, just as she does in advertising. Genesis 2–3 serves didactic purposes and one of them is to suggest the danger of a woman allowed to have authority.[15]

Carey Ellen Walsh also argues that mainstream traditional interpretations of the text, following Augustine, were plucked from the air and certainly not from the biblical text:

> Augustine managed to link desire, sex and shame in a slam dunk of guilt-inducing interpretation. The biblical problem, of course, is that desire is the only element mentioned in the text. Sex is nowhere evident, and shame is a rather strong inference to draw from the couple's new-found awareness of their nakedness.[16]

But could one not argue that Augustine and many who followed him were picking up on hints, suggestions and meanings latent in the text? It is difficult to maintain that there is no sex in this text or that centuries of misogynist readings alone are to blame for Eve's bad reputation and the sexist treatment meted out to generations of women. For instance, contrary to Walsh's argument, shame is not 'a rather strong inference to draw from the couple's new-found awareness of their nakedness' but a perfectly logical one. Before the transgression the couple are naked and not ashamed (Gen. 2.25). After the transgression their eyes are opened. They know they are naked and therefore sew fig-leaves together to cover themselves (3.7). This seems to indicate that the pair are ashamed, or at the very least embarrassed, of being naked, whether the shame they feel is shame in front of each other or before God, as Fewell and Gunn conclude:

> The man and the woman know nakedness and shame (Genesis 3:7, 10-11; cf. 2:25). The knowledge of sexual difference brings shame in its train. Sex and shame. That association, however, primarily serves the interest of the party wanting sexual control—that is, men who want to control women's sexuality.[17]

---

15. I am not suggesting that the only didactic purpose of the story is to warn of the peril of women and certainly not that the story is only about the danger of female sexuality. What I am suggesting is that these readings are entirely plausible and that the text lends itself to androcentric interpretation.

16. Walsh, *Exquisite Desire*, p. 153.

17. Danna Nolan Fewell and David M. Gunn, *Gender, Power, and Promise: The Subject of the Bible's First Story* (Nashville: Abingdon Press, 1993), p. 26.

The couple go from being naked and unashamed before the transgression to the realization that they are naked and covering that nakedness after the episode. Shame is an interpretation of what motivates Adam and Eve to cover themselves after they recognize nakedness after previously being naked and unashamed.

I do not share the confidence of scholars such as Trible and Kimelman that Genesis 2–3 is an egalitarian text. This is not to say that an egalitarian reading of the text is not possible. It can even be quite persuasive, as David Clines comments in his criticism of Trible's analysis of the text;[18] however, there are many reasons not to view this text as egalitarian. Popular culture knows it is not egalitarian, and the imbalance of power in the text is exactly what leads advertisers to turn the tables on traditional male dominance in the story and re-read it as female dominance, the subjugation of the male through irresistible female sexuality. Moreover, one could argue that male dominance is a thread that runs through the biblical text even before the transgression in Genesis 3.

It Is Not Good that the Man Should Be Alone

God creates a companion for the first human being, referred to in the text as *ha'adam*, because, God decides (the man has nothing to do with it), 'it is not good that *ha'adam* should be alone' (2.18). What is the nature of this companion? The answer to this question depends upon what one understands to be the nature of *ha'adam*. Is the first creature sexually undifferentiated, androgynous or male?[19] Scholars such as Trible, Kimelman and Bal have argued that *ha'adam* describes a sexually undifferentiated earth creature, whereas others, such as Clines, Lanser and Milne, have argued that *ha'adam* refers to a male.

Trible's argument that *ha'adam* is an earth creature is based on the premise that, although the grammatical gender of the word is male, the term does not refer to a male, but is a generic term for humankind. Thus she translates *ha'adam* as 'earth creature'.[20] God creates a woman from

---

18. David Clines, *What Does Eve Do to Help? And Other Readerly Questions to the Old Testament* (Sheffield: JSOT Press, 1990), p. 29.

19. Trible is at pains to point out that the first creature is not a sexual being and thus distinguishes between a sexually undifferentiated creature and an androgynous being. Contemporary scholars have tended to follow Trible in arguing for a sexually undifferentiated being as opposed to one that is androgynous, that is, both male and female. This distinction is not particularly relevant for the debate, since the key point is whether or not a male is created first and a female later.

20. Trible, *God and the Rhetoric of Sexuality*, pp. 79-82.

part of this earth creature and what remains is a man. After the woman is created, what was once a marker for humanity without sexual differentiation now becomes a sexual reference for the male, and the couple is referred to as *ha'adam* and his woman. This is a weakness in Trible's argument. After the woman is created *ha'adam* says 'she shall be called woman (*'ishshah*) because she was taken out of man' (*'ish*). For Trible's argument to be convincing, one would expect the story from this point on to refer to the man (*'ish*) and his woman (*'ishshah*) but the text refers to them as *ha'adam* and his woman (*'ishshah*). The repetition of *ha'adam* after the splitting of the sexes suggests that the 'earth creature' was, in fact, male after all. In favour of Trible's argument is the fact that at the end of the story, in 3.24, we are told that God drove *ha'adam* out of the garden. Here we must assume that *ha'adam* is used as a collective, to refer to the man and the woman. It must include the woman, otherwise the woman would still be in the garden. By applying speech-act theory to the biblical text, Susan Lanser offers a persuasive argument against Trible that the earth creature is sexually undifferentiated:

> This understanding of language implies that meaning is created not only by decoding signs but by drawing on contextual assumptions to make inferences. That is, every act of understanding relies (unconsciously and sometimes also consciously) on complex rules and assumptions about social and cultural behaviour and language use...within such a framework communication is a function not only of signifiers but silences; meaning is not coextensive with words on-a-page but is constituted by the performance of the text in a context which teems with culture-specific linguistic rules that are almost never articulated.[21]

Taking into account the social and cultural context within which a text is created and read, Lanser concludes that the original audience would have understood the first creature to be male.

> When a being assumed to be human is introduced into a narrative, that being is also assumed to have sexual as well as grammatical gender. The masculine form of *ha'adam* and its associated pronoun will, by inference, define *ha'adam* as male. I am not suggesting that one cannot read *ha'adam* as a sex-neutral figure; I am saying that readers will not ordinarily read Genesis 2–3 in this way. Gendered humans are the unmarked case; it is not *ha'adam*'s maleness that would have to be marked but the absence of maleness.[22]

21. Susan Lanser, '(Feminist) Criticism in the Garden: Inferring Genesis 2–3', in Hugh C. White (ed.), *Speech Act Theory and Biblical Criticism* (Semeia, 41; Atlanta: Scholars Press, 1987), pp. 67-84 (70).
22. Lanser, '(Feminist) Criticism in the Garden', p. 70.

Lanser's argument, unlike Trible's, takes more seriously into account the patriarchal culture in which this text was written. It is unlikely that a patriarchal text would disavow patriarchy by promoting egalitarianism.

As the many biblical scholars involved in the *ha'adam* debate have found, there is no way to prove conclusively either that the term refers to a male or to a sexually undifferentiated earth creature or collective. The answer to this question, however, has little bearing on the argument of this book. My contention is that regardless of whether humanity was egalitarian at the start of the story, by the time the woman is created the hierarchy of genders is implied in the text through the woman's role of helper and her absence of voice in Genesis 2, both of which will be discussed below.

I Will Make for Him a Helper Fit for Him

It is God who decides that *ha'adam*—and from this point I will be referring to him as the man—should not be alone. After it transpires that none of the animals is a suitable helper, God creates a woman from the side of the man. Does her creation from the man imply subordination? For centuries this is the way it has been understood. Trible, however, argues that the term 'helper' in Hebrew ('*ezer*) does not imply inferior rank, as the term does in English.[23] She argues that the term is neutral. God in the Bible is referred to as a helper, and he is superior to humans. The animals in this story are helpers and they are inferior to the man. Central for Trible's argument is her understanding of the preposition *kenegdo*, traditionally translated 'fit for him', as meaning 'corresponding to him' and implying equal rank. This rather begs the issue, for regardless of how we translate the preposition, a problem remains with the meaning of the word 'helper'.

As Clines shows, the term 'helper' is not a helper in the sense of a 'companion' or a 'partner' that is an equal.

> What I conclude, from reviewing all the occurrences in the Hebrew Bible, is that though superiors may help inferiors, strong may help weak, gods may help humans, in the act of helping they are being 'inferior'. That is to say, they are subjecting themselves to a secondary, subordinate position. Their help may be necessary or crucial, but they are *assisting* some task that is already someone else's responsibility. They are not actually *doing* the task themselves, or even in cooperation, for there is different language for that.[24]

---

23. Trible, *God and the Rhetoric of Sexuality*, pp. 88-89.
24. Clines, *What Does Eve Do to Help?*, pp. 30-31.

Another male could have been created to be the man's helper. Why, asks Clines, should a different sex be created for this role? What does Eve do to help? The answer, as Clines persuasively argues, is that the woman is created to help the man with procreation. As Clines observes, 'This view of Eve's helpfulness also explains the narrative's emphasis on nakedness, on the man cleaving to the woman, and on their being one flesh'.[25] The man recognizes her as the 'right' helper because she is bone of his bone and flesh of his flesh (Gen. 2.23), and, consequently, a man will leave his parents so that he can have a sexual relationship with his woman. Eve is created as a sexual partner for Adam, and even Kimelman cannot rescue her from her lot when he suggests that:

> Chapter 2 explicitly states that the splitting of *ha'adam* comes to resolve the problem of loneliness, a problem more likely to be resolved by a counterpart than a helper. This role for woman also matches the part she plays in ch.3, a part that resembles more that of male complement than that of helper in any subordinate sense.[26]

Kimelman fails to explain why it was necessary to introduce another sex if Eve is made only solve the problems of Adam's loneliness. Moreover, Eve is not presented as a counterpart to the man in the narrative, but as his supporting act. The Church Fathers, it seems, were not far off the mark with their interpretations. The seeds of the idea that the function of woman is as sexual mate to man are already sown in the text before the transgression takes place. After the transgression the punishments or consequences reinforce the gendered roles assigned to the couple. Adam still has the task of working the ground and Eve remains a child-bearing vessel and sexual partner for Adam:

> To the woman he said,
> 'I will greatly increase your pangs in
>   childbearing;
> in pain you shall bring forth children,
> yet your desire shall be for your husband,
> and he shall rule over you'.
> And to the man, he said,
> 'Because you have listened to the voice
>   of your wife,
> and eaten from the tree,
> about which I commanded you,
> you shall not eat of it,
> cursed is the ground because of you;

25. Clines, *What Does Eve Do to Help?*, p. 35.
26. Kimelman, 'The Seduction of Eve and the Exegetical Politics of Gender', p. 16.

in toil you shall eat of it all the days
   of your life;
thorns and thistles it shall bring forth
   for you;
and you shall eat the plants of the field.
By the sweat of your face
you shall eat bread
until you return to the ground,
for out of it you were taken;
you are dust,
and to dust you shall return' (Gen. 3.16-20).

The punishments do not serve to change Adam and Eve's prescribed roles by bringing disruption to the 'harmony and unity' seen in Genesis 2 as Trible argues,[27] but instead serve to make Adam and Eve's assigned social roles more difficult. Adam is associated with the ground from which he was taken while Eve is associated with the body and sexuality. Eve was taken from Adam's body to fulfil a sexual function and her punishments echo both her origin, by linking her with the body again, and her social function as sexual partner to Adam. She will be subjugated by him but will desire him and her body will feel great pain because of her sexual function, or, as Clines wryly observes:

> It is also clear that God regards Eve as primarily a child-bearing creature… [A]fter the sin of the couple he does not punish the woman by threatening her with demotion to intellectual inferiority or by rendering her incapable of keeping up interesting conversation with her partner, but he most severely punishes her by promising to make the one thing she has been created to do difficult for her… [J]ust as Adam will find his work as farmer painful, so she will find hers as mother.[28]

The man's punishment is preceded by the statement, 'because you have obeyed the voice of your wife,[29] and have eaten from the tree about which I commanded you, you shall not eat of it'. This information comes as something of a surprise. Nothing was said earlier about 'obeying' or 'listening to' the woman's voice, but clearly, now, the woman is blamed as the instigator of the transgression. It should therefore come as no surprise that she has been blamed by readers ever since. Here the reader learns that Adam should not have obeyed the voice of his wife. God

---

27. Trible, *God and the Rhetoric of Sexuality*, pp. 115-39.
28. Clines, *What Does Eve Do to Help?*, p. 35.
29. The typical translation 'you have listened to the voice of your wife' does not convey the force of the Hebrew idiom *shema' beqol*, which is better translated 'obey' (see Francis Brown, S.R. Driver and Charles A. Briggs, *A Hebrew and English Lexicon of the Old Testament* [Oxford: Clarendon Press, 1907], p. 1034a).

gives Adam a sentence of hard labour for his folly of following the actions of his wife. For her part, the woman is subjugated to the man—an extension of the gender hierarchy hinted at in Genesis 2. The encoded message in the text is that women need to be subjugated and controlled by men. The text teaches men that the consequences of letting woman have power are dangerous. Adam is officially promoted in the gender league in a bizarre twist to the tale that sees Adam's elevated social status confirmed and his dominant role amplified. Although it was implied earlier in the text that Adam was superior to Eve, it is now made explicit.

Because You Have Obeyed the Voice of Your Wife

In Genesis 2, far from evidence of parity there is evidence of the gender hierarchy that will be developed in the transgression consequences in Gen. 3.12-24. There can be no doubt that the woman makes a great silent partner for Adam; she gives her crucial support to his role in order for it to be successful but has no active input.[30] In Genesis 2, Adam names all the cattle, the birds of the air and every animal in the field (2.20). He offers his opinion on his new 'helper' when she is brought to him (2.23). He decides what she will be called:

> This at last is bone of my bones
> and flesh of my flesh;
> this one shall be called Woman,
> for out of Man this one was taken.

Eve says nothing. We know that Adam is happy with her, but we do not know what she thinks about Adam or if she is happy with her helper status. Adam has a choice over what, or who, is to be his 'helper', and he refuses all the other creatures, finding satisfaction only with the woman born out of his own body. The woman, however, is given no choice and no voice:

> Upon meeting her new companion, would she have been impressed? Disappointed? Ambivalent? But such possibilities of subjectivity are avoided, suppressed. We might easily infer that were she to have opinions they would not, in any case, matter—not to God, the man, or the narrator. Men can have opinions about women (the objects of male desire: Genesis 2:24), but women's perceptions of men are not important.[31]

---

30. Clines argues along the same lines when he comments: 'Whether the helper is superior or not will depend entirely on other factors, extrinsic to the relationship constituted by the act of helping'. *What Does Eve Do to Help?*, p. 31.

31. Fewell and Gunn, *Gender, Power, and Promise*, p. 29.

After Genesis 2, where the woman is more of a supporting act to the man than a counterpart, comes Genesis 3, when Eve suddenly turns into the star of the show. Where has this assertive, outspoken woman come from? This is the episode that popular culture portrays in its representations of Adam and Eve. Eve and her eating of the fruit and her giving of the fruit to Adam bring about a radical change from the final verse of the last chapter, 'The man and his wife were both naked and not ashamed', to the surprising revelation in chap. 3, 'then the eyes of both were opened, and they knew that they were naked; and they sewed fig leaves together and made clothes for themselves'. In Genesis 3 Eve is the active character and Adam passive. In the build up to, and at the moment of transgression, Adam has no narrative presence: the dialogue and the action are left to Eve. Why should Adam suddenly become silent in the text? Is this the biblical narrator's way of subtly removing him from direct responsibility for eating the forbidden fruit? His role is so small that we discover he is there only in v. 6, when we are told 'and she also gave some to her husband, who was with her, and he ate'. Adam's apparently minor role helps us to understand how popular advertising has preferred an interpretation according to which Eve has a dominant role in the narrative. Eve has the larger role in the transgression episode and, thanks to Adam's lack of presence in the scene, the blame for eating the forbidden fruit is left at her feet. Advertisers accept this picture. But in contrast to the biblical narrator, who portrays Eve's transgression as justification of the subordination of women to men, advertisers turn on its head the notion that Eve's main role in the transgression episode is the cause of her subjugation and depict the temptation as the source of her power and the cause of the man's subjugation instead.

Both humans eat the fruit. They are both the cause of their expulsion from Eden, but do they both transgress equally, as many commentators would have us think?[32] The narrator, by giving more narrative space to Eve's actions and deliberations than to Adam's, implies that she deserves the guilt or blame for eating the forbidden fruit. Leaving Adam without a voice at the crucial moment of the temptation has the effect of making Adam look like a weakling. As readers we should wonder why Gen. 3.1-7 awards so much more narrative space to Eve's actions and deliberations than to Adam's. After all, he was with her. Why did Adam not speak up

32. See Trible, 'A Love Story Gone Awry', pp. 72-143; Kimelman, 'The Seduction of Eve and the Exegetical Politics of Gender'; Bal, *Lethal Love*; and Carol L. Meyers, *Discovering Eve: Ancient Israelite Woman in Context* (Oxford: Oxford University Press, 1988), pp. 72-94.

and tell Eve that they were not supposed to eat from *this* tree? Why did he not raise any objections or make any comment about what the serpent said? Adam is kept out of the picture until the end of the episode in order to make him look less guilty at Eve's expense.

Advertisers focus exclusively on the moment of transgression, picking up on textual clues to the woman's central role and her guilt. In this advertisement for the Brazilian handbag manufacturer Chenson, for example, although both Eve and Adam hold the bitten fruit together and Adam is part of the picture, he is disengaged from the situation and from the viewer, indicating his lack of responsibility for the episode (Fig. 1.4). Eve, in contrast, makes eye contact with the viewer: she is offering the apple as much to us as she is to Adam.

Figure 1.4. *Print advertisement for Chenson Handbags, 2010*[33]

It seems that popular culture takes its cue from the biblical text and removes responsibility from Adam, placing it upon a knowing, seductive Eve. How can we blame Adam for buckling under the pressure of Eve's considerable charms?

The text is structured so that it appears that Eve *does* transgress to a greater extent than Adam. He has no narrative presence in the episode except for the passage, 'and she also gave some to her husband, who was

33.   Upon the release of this series of advertisements for the Autumn 2010 advertising campaign, the Chenson brand received considerable press attention for its choice of the theme of temptation and the models cast in the starring roles: Victoria's Secret model Alessandro Ambrosio and Jesus Luz, Madonna's 23 year old ex-boyfriend.

with her, and he ate' (Gen. 3.6), which occurs after Eve has been described talking to the serpent and eating the fruit. Of course, the text contains within it the seeds of its own ideological deconstruction because Eve exposes the vulnerability of those in power. If it is such an easy task to divert the man enough to jeopardize the future of paradise merely by being naked and offering fruit, then patriarchy seems, to me at least, to be treading on very thin ice. As David Jobling comments:

> Part of the price the male mindset pays is the admission that woman is more aware of the complexity of the world, more in touch with 'all living'. And finally, at the deepest level of the text...the possibility is evoked that the human transformation in which the woman took powerful initiative was positive, rather than negative, that the complex human world is to be preferred over any male ideal. But these 'positive' features are not the direct expression of a feminist consciousness... Rather, they are the effects of the patriarchal mindset tying itself in knots trying to account for woman and femaleness in a way which both makes sense and supports patriarchal assumptions.[34]

For popular cultural postfeminist interpretations of the biblical story, this vulnerability of male authority to loss of power and status through the irresistible allure of women means that the text is an ideal sales ground for products intended to increase women's sexual attractiveness and, therefore, social power—the reason that advertisements tend to portray only the moment of transgression or directly after. Genesis 3.1-7 is the only passage in the text in which Eve exercises any power and the only passage in which she is afforded a point of view by the narrator. Popular culture, seeking a postfeminist heroine, would not find her in Genesis 2 and certainly not after the transgression, when God metes out the punishments to the man and the woman for eating the fruit.

And She also Gave Some to Her Husband Who Was with Her

I asked above, with regard to the temptation scene, why Eve suddenly becomes so vocal. Alice Bach offers some help here:

> While culinary codes and banquet settings are not found in the majority of biblical narratives, they are important to mark transitions within the life-cycle, alterations in the expected role of a character, or interplays of sexual desire and possible danger.[35]

---

34. David Jobling, *The Sense of Biblical Narrative. II. Structural Analyses in the Hebrew Bible* (Sheffield: JSOT Press, 1986), pp. 42-43 (emphasis original).

35. Alice Bach, *Women, Seduction and Betrayal in Biblical Narrative* (Cambridge: Cambridge University Press, 1997), p. 183.

The moment of transgression, when Eve discusses the fruit with the serpent, fits what Bach says about culinary codes. Eve's taking of the fruit marks the transition from 'naked and unashamed' (Gen. 2.25, which appears directly before the transgression episode in chap. 3) to 'naked and covered' (Gen. 3.7, which appears directly after the transgression episode). Also, since the man and the woman reverse the expected active male/passive female gender roles for the transgression episode, the eating of the fruit marks the change in the woman's role from silent 'helper' to primary actor and the change in the man's role from an active and vocal character to a passive follower, fulfilling another one of Bach's functions of culinary codes in the biblical text: to mark the alterations in the expected role of a character. This leaves us with 'interplays of sexual desire and possible danger'. Is it a coincidence that fruit is the article of transgression? Is it a coincidence that at the moment of transgression it is a naked woman who thinks for herself who offers forbidden food (fruit no less) to the man? Nakedness may mean many things, among them vulnerability, but it would be a rare reader who would not also associate it with sexuality, especially female sexuality.[36] Not only nakedness but also food is part of the female arsenal signifying sensuality and desire. In addition, food belongs to the feminine domain, and, as such, it is a means by which women can appropriate power from men.[37] For women without access to other avenues of obtaining power, food has been a way to exploit the methods that are available to them.[38]

Countless readers across the centuries have interpreted Eve's potent female sexuality as the reason for Adam's lack of resistance to Eve's offering him the fruit. There is some basis in the biblical text for such an interpretation. Some arguments have been put forth for understanding the phrase 'good and evil' as a reference to sexual intercourse,[39] though

36. See Margaret R. Miles, *Carnal Knowing: Female Nakedness and Religious Meaning in the Christian West* (Kent: Burns & Oates, 1992), for an extensive discussion on the various meanings of nakedness in Western culture.

37. Bach goes on to say, 'In the majority of biblical narratives dealing with food, as I read them, the food is seasoned with the sexual power of woman. It is a connection of pleasure and power, a connection that too often leads to death for the man who trusts the offering'; Alice Bach, 'Eating their Words', in Athalya Brenner and Jan Willem van Henten (eds.), *Food and Drink in the Biblical World* (Semeia, 86; Atlanta: Society of Biblical Literature, 1999), pp. 215-22 (220).

38. See Stewart Lee Allen, *In the Devil's Garden: A Sinful History of Forbidden Food* (Edinburgh: Canongate Books, 2002).

39. See Ronald A. Veenker, 'Forbidden Fruit: Ancient Near Eastern Sexual Metaphors', *Hebrew Union College Annual* 70–71 (1999–2000), pp. 53-73. There is no

this is not the most likely explanation.[40] Perhaps it is a merismus meaning 'everything',[41] but this is not an entirely satisfactory explanation either. The phrase remains something of a mystery.

Regardless of the meaning of the phrase 'good and evil' to describe the effect of eating the fruit, it still raises the question of a possible relationship between food and sex. Fruit, for example, is used to describe female sexuality in the Song of Songs, and this is a code that has not lost its significance in the contemporary world.[42] The forbidden fruit comes to symbolize sex, as Figures 1.5–1.8 illustrate.

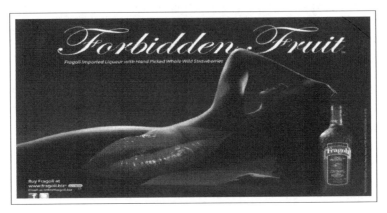

Figure 1.5. *Print advertisement for Fragoli Wild Strawberry Liqueur, 2008*

specific mention of sexual intercourse until 4.1 after the couple has eaten; the verb *yada'* frequently has a sexual meaning; the serpent has phallic significance in the ancient Near East; the scene is a garden, suggesting a fertility setting; there is an interesting parallel in the Gilgamesh Epic, when, after sexual intercourse, the harlot says to Enkidu, 'you are wise, Enkidu, you have become like a god'.

40.   One could assume sexual intercourse from 2.24; the verb *yada'* in a sexual sense has a clear sexual object. Moreover, in 3.22 God says that 'the man has become like one of us, knowing good and evil' and God, for the biblical writers, is not a sexual being; also, the woman eats first then the man.

41.   Gerhard von Rad, *Genesis: A Commentary* (Philadelphia: Westminster Press, 1972), p. 55.

42.   See a variety of books on this subject for comprehensive enquiries into the food/sex connection in contemporary culture (all of which mention the Gen. 2–3 account as a literary example of this link between food and eroticism): Smith, *Hungry for You;* Cristina Moles Kaupp, *The Erotic Cookbook* (London: Fusion Press, 2002); Martha Hopkins and Randall Lockridge, *New Intercourses: An Aphrodisiac Cookbook* (London: Terrace Publishing, 2007); Amy Reiley, *Fork Me, Spoon Me: The Sensual Cookbook* (London: Life of Reiley, 2010); Isabel Allende, *Aphrodite: The Love of Food and the Food of Love* (London: Harper Perennial, 2010), and Allen, *In the Devil's Garden,* to name but a few on this currently very popular topic.

Figure 1.6. *Print advertisement for Pink Lady apples, 2005*

Figure 1.7. *Print advertisement for Nomad Lounge New Years Eve Party, 2007*

Figure 1.8. *Second page of promotional brochure*
for True Religion underwear, 2000

As these images show, it is almost always female sexuality that is identified with the fruit in mainstream advertising. In the first image (Fig. 1.5),
an ad for Fragoli Wild Strawberry liqueur, a lipsticked kiss, echoing the
same shade of red as the liqueur, is imposed on the naked back of a
woman's reclining body. Figure 1.6 similarly associates the promise of
female sexuality with forbidden fruit to make the prospect of getting the
recommended five-a-day fresh fruit and vegetable portions seem more
tantalising to the consumer. In the third, most explicit image (Fig. 1.7),
a nightclub's New Years Eve party is promoted by representing the
sexualized female body *as* the forbidden fruit. The fourth image, a page of
a promotional brochure for underwear (Fig. 1.8), shows the illicit effect
of the underwear by depicting two nuns who have apparently eaten the
forbidden fruit (associated with the apparent sexiness of the underwear)
and turned 'bad'. Their knowing expression is emphasized by the cropping of the image so that just their eyes and habits are visible, and they
wear heavy eye make-up, which sexualizes them.

In advertising images, as in the biblical text, it is the woman, Eve, as
the one who decides to eat the fruit, who is more strongly identified with
the forbidden fruit than the man, Adam. In the popular cultural imagination the temptation offered by the fruit becomes the temptation
offered by woman. Women in Western popular culture are constructed as

the desired, the object of the gaze, the forbidden fruit pleasing to the eye and displayed for temptation. Popular culture has recognized this aspect of the biblical story long before some feminist biblical scholars began to accept that Genesis 2–3 is an irredeemably androcentric text, and it is this interpretation of the text that advertisers are currently exploiting by turning the story of Adam and Eve's transgression into a postfeminist tale of female victory through influential sexuality. As a result of her starring role in the transgression, and not least due to the fact that the transgression involves a naked woman giving her partner forbidden fruit to eat, Eve becomes a postfeminist capitalist heroine.

In the text too, fruit has connotations of female sexuality. This is not to say that the fruit functions only as a symbol of female sexuality, for symbolic meaning is complex, but one can posit a connection between women's bodies and sex in the biblical temptation account. Carey Ellen Walsh makes a perceptive and persuasive case for the deep connection between food and sex in her analysis of the Song of the Songs,[43] a text that has many similarities to Genesis 2–3:[44] 'They [fruit] are symbols of succulent enjoyment, markers of sensual pleasure… [F]ruit gave alimentary pleasure and also came to represent other sensual delights.'[45] Furthermore, she observes, 'Horticulture simply and powerfully summons the oral excitement in sexual pleasure, then and now'.[46] She goes on:

> The excitement of desire is an orgiastic inundation of all our senses with taste at the forefront, and this is why food and sex are so often associated in our imaginings of sensual pleasure. Both food and sex stimulate the mouth and cater to the orality of pleasure.[47]

Curiously, considering the amount of space Walsh devotes to the function of fruit as a sexual symbol in the biblical text, she fails to analyse the function of the fruit in Genesis 2–3 at all. She seems to undermine her argument for the carnality of fruit as a literary trope by denying that Eve and the transgression have any connection with sex. Despite a long and detailed account of the link between eroticism, sex, fruit and desire, Walsh considers there to be no link between Adam and Eve's eating of the fruit and sex.[48] Walsh states:

43. Walsh, 'The Orality of Desire', in *Exquisite Desire*, pp. 114-29.
44. See Trible, 'Love's Lyrics Redeemed', in *God and the Rhetoric of Sexuality*, pp. 144-65, and Francis Landy, *Paradoxes of Paradise: Identity and Difference in the Song of Songs* (Sheffield: Almond Press, 1983).
45. Walsh, *Exquisite Desire*, p. 117.
46. Walsh, *Exquisite Desire*, p. 118.
47. Walsh, *Exquisite Desire*, p. 119.
48. Walsh, *Exquisite Desire*, p. 129.

Eve exercised desire for both wisdom and fruit, and this desire was then cursed
by being redirected to her husband. That this story came to associate woman
and sexuality with sin is a notorious post-biblical development. Eve became
the scapegoat for a culture's anxieties about the body, sexuality and women.[49]

If food and sex are closely connected, and if ancient and contemporary
readers so readily interpret fruit as 'symbols of sexual delight', then why
does this argument not extend to Genesis 2–3 for Walsh? Fruit in
Genesis 2–3 represents what is forbidden, nakedness suggests female
sexuality and becomes associated with forbidden fruit. From there it is a
short step for advertisers to adopt fruit as a symbol of sexual temptation
on the part of women. The fact is, readers *have* interpreted the fruit as a
sexual symbol, whatever the ancient author might have intended.[50]

The traditional perception of Eve as sexual temptress, then, shows no
sign of dwindling appeal for the consumer. Since she has evolved into a
cultural icon, it is unlikely that she will ever break free from her mould.
After all, Eve is quite a money-maker, and so long as she can bring in the
revenue she will be out there in cinemas and magazines with her trusty
apple and snake to lure in the consumers to take a bite of whatever product she is selling. Both advertisers and consumers love Eve's assertive,
sexy, forbidden fruit-offering character, and, conveniently for advertisers
wishing to target the much desired young female consumer market, the
transgression of Genesis 3 can be re-read through a postfeminist lens as a
story of female sexuality turning the tables on traditional male dominance: the subjugation of the male through irresistible female sexuality.
The fruit is essential to this postfeminist equation; it represents empowered female sexuality, highly attractive to men but no longer under their
control, or so the purveyors of pop culture would have us believe.[51] In the
next chapter we will see that the experiences of many modern-day
women, however, may tell a different story.

49. Walsh, *Exquisite Desire*, p. 152.
50. See Smith, *Hungry for You*, and Allen, *In the Devil's Garden*, for numerous examples of the ways in which women have been equated with forbidden fruit in Western
culture.
51. See Chapter 2 for a discussion of how young women continue to be sexually
disempowered in heterosexual relationships despite claims to the contrary from popular
culture.

2

THE NEVER-CHANGING FACE OF EVE: REPRESENTATIONS OF EVE IN NINETEENTH-CENTURY FIN-DE-SIÈCLE ART AND TWENTIETH-CENTURY FIN-DE-SIÈCLE ADVERTISING

To enjoy women at all, one must manufacture an illusion and envelop them with it, otherwise they would not be so endurable.

—George Jean Nathan, 1929

The most effective lure that a woman can hold out to a man is the lure of what he fatuously conceives to be her beauty.

—H.L. Mencken, 1924

When Eve once knew *in her mind* that she was naked
She quickly sewed fig-leaves, and sewed the same for the man.
She'd been naked all her days before,
But till then, till that apple of knowledge, she hadn't had the fact on her mind.

She got the fact on her mind, and quickly sewed fig-leaves.
And women have been sewing ever since.
But now they stitch to adorn the bursten fig, not to cover it.
They have their nakedness more than ever on their mind,
And they won't let us forget it.

—D.H. Lawrence, 1923

The final decade of the twentieth century saw a revival of interest in the culturally notorious image of Eve, the temptress. Marketed as the ulti-mate example of the power of audacious female sexuality, Eve embodied the *Zeitgeist* of an era in which postfeminism reigned: 'girl power' was celebrated by the Spice Girls and their fans, 'kick-ass babes' like Charlie's Angels got to hit men where it hurt while sporting various fetish outfits[1]

1. *Charlie's Angels* (Sony Pictures Home Entertainment UK, 2000) and the sequel *Charlie's Angels 2: Full Throttle* (Sony Pictures Home Entertainment UK, 2003), both directed by McG, were both highly profitable for Sony. Despite being criticized in

and girls of twelve wore T-shirts that claimed 'This Bitch Bites'.[2] The last time there was such an interest in Eve was at the end of the nineteenth century when the image was also widespread. It is no accident that there has been a resurgence of popular representations of Eve at the end of the twentieth century because her image has been a particularly convenient symbol for similar social circumstances in each period. Whereas at the end of the nineteenth century images of Eve were ubiquitous in art, at the end of the twentieth century her image is prevalent in advertising.

This chapter looks at the way that the image of Eve, as sexual tempt-ress, was exploited as a symbol of each era's idea of womanhood for differ-ent ends. Detailed accounts of the *femme fatale* in all its manifestations in the nineteenth-century fin-de-siècle can be found in important works by Elaine Showalter, Virginia Allen, Patrick Bade, Elizabeth Menon, Jennifer Hedgecock, Joseph Kestner, Helen Hanson and Catherine O'Rawe and Rebecca Stott.[3] Each century's image of Eve reflects the socio-political climate of the time, yet they are remarkably similar. My argument here is that the threat of feminism is a major, if not the major, social factor underlying the birth and rebirth of the image of woman as *femme fatale*, and that the proliferation of Eve images in each fin-de siècle is a cultural response aimed at managing this threat by appealing to deep-rooted prejudices about the biblical figure of Eve. A comparative

reviews for objectifying the female characters in the film, due to the frequent and lingering camera shots on the body parts of the actresses, the majority of the audience for the films was female and under 30, illustrating that the objectification of women in popular culture is now a way of targeting a young female audience rather than the traditionally male audience that this type of film would once have attracted. The success of the *Charlie's Angels* franchise (the twenty-first-century filmic version rather than the 1970s TV series) with young women prompted the actress Cameron Diaz, who played an Angel in both films, to comment that the film was 'holding a mirror up to women and reflecting who they are now'. Interview in *Glamour*, July 2000 issue.

  2.   See Anita M. Harris, *Future Girl: Young Women in the Twenty-First Century* (London: Routledge, 2004), for a comprehensive analysis of the fashion, behaviour and issues of girls and young women in twenty-first-century Western culture.

  3.   Elaine Showalter, *Sexual Anarchy: Gender and Culture at the Fin-de-siècle* (London: Bloomsbury, 1991); Virginia M. Allen, *The Femme Fatale: Erotic Icon* (Troy, NY: Whitston Publishing, 1983); Patrick Bade, *Femme Fatale: Images of Evil and Fascinat-ing Women* (New York: Mayflower Books, 1979); Menon, *Evil by Design*; Jennifer Hedgecock, *The Femme Fatale in Victorian Literature: The Danger and the Sexual Threat* (New York: Cambria Press, 2008); Joseph Kestner, *Mythology and Misogyny: The Social Discourse of Nineteenth Century British Classical-Subject Painting* (Madison: University of Wisconsin Press, 1989); Helen Hanson and Catherine O'Rawe (eds.), *The Femme Fatale: Images, Histories, Contexts* (Hampshire: Palgrave Macmillan, 2010); Rebecca Stott, *The Fabrication of the Late-Victorian Femme Fatale: The Kiss of Death* (London: Macmillan Press, 1992).

overview of every way in which the social issues of the fin-de-siècle eras of the nineteenth and twentieth centuries were similar or dissimilar is beyond the scope of this book,[4] but each era faced social issues, the most burning of which centred around changes in sexual behaviour and challenges to traditional gender relations, whose impact on the fin-de-siècle societies was increased in intensity by the apocalyptic panic of the end of century. As Elaine Showalter explains in her book, *Sexual Anarchy*, parallels between the two, most recent, fin-de-siècle eras can be drawn, not only in terms of the shared *femme fatale* imagery produced by nineteenth-century artists and twentieth-century popular culture but also in the parallels that can be drawn between the perceived social issues addressed and reflected in this imagery.

In both fin-de-siècle eras the female body is presented as the locus of their socio-sexual upheaval. The female and her sexuality were something to be feared. For each era, Eve was the most popular *femme fatale* icon (along with Salome and Greek mythological characters in 1890's art) to represent the socio-sexual climate because she symbolizes female autonomy and its dangers. When artists of the 1890s use images of Eve, they show her as a source of death and degeneration.[5] In the twentieth century, when the *femme fatale* again became popular, the image of Eve was recycled by translating the older image of misogyny into one of empowerment for today's postfeminist 'I'm not a feminist but...' generation. When the nineteenth-century artist represented his fear of the 'New Woman' with images of the *femme fatale*, the animalistic, overtly sexual, temptress women, as a warning of the perils of female sexuality— especially unfettered female sexuality—twentieth-century pop culture recycled those images for a society where the 'New Woman' was apparently revelling in her feminine power. Feminism, apparently defunct now that equality has been achieved, is replaced by postfeminism, where female sexuality, once controlled by men, is now viewed as in the control of women themselves and the New Woman can have it all: sexual and financial independence, power in gender relations and the body image of your choice.

4.   In addition to the challenges brought by epidemics of sexually transmitted diseases and feminism discussed in this chapter, parallels in issues of immigration, blurring of racial and sexual boundaries (in respect to homosexuality) and the belief that the perceived breakdown of society was caused by the breakdown of the traditional family unit and miscegenation can be made between the nineteenth- and twentieth-century fin-de-siècles; again, Showalter's book on fin-de-siècle, *Sexual Anarchy*, addresses these issues.

5.   For specific examples see below, where I compare the 1890 paintings with contemporary advertisements.

In this climate, images of Eve represent the ultimate postfeminist. She exercises her power through her female sexuality, which is maintained or boosted though her consumer spending power—the greater the consumer power, the greater the power of her sexuality to increase her social status, or so the images would have today's young women believe. For the post-feminist target consumer, these images of Eve are a celebration of the sexual autonomy and financial independence for which the nineteenth-century suffragettes had fought. The contemporary young female target consumers, however, have more in common with the nineteenth-century woman than postfeminist advertising would have them imagine. Whereas the nineteenth century had to deal with the syphilis epidemic, in the final decade of the twentieth century society was reeling from the blow of AIDS. The nineteenth century wrestled with worries of an uncertain future labour economy as a result of the New Woman making moves to become the Employed Woman (although in reality the effect of the New Woman on the job market was minimal to say the least). At the end of the twentieth century and beginning of the twenty-first century, the fashion for conspicuous consumerism, soaring house prices, rates of infla-tion and the cost of living caused widespread insolvency, creating the global economic crisis of 2007–10. If the Odd Woman—a term used to describe the steadily increasing surplus of unmarried women in England— of the late nineteenth-century was derided for her refusal to fulfil her duty of motherhood, the late twentieth-century woman was being casti-gated by a scare-mongering media, which, in reaction to the sharply rising rates of thirty-plus mothers and women who more frequently chose career over motherhood, warned that she was ruining her own life and mental and physical health as well as risking the birth replacement rates of the country.[6] In other words, although the *femme fatale* Eve images

6.   See this sample of newspaper headlines and popular books published from 2000–2011, which illustrate this anxiety with delayed/early/working motherhood and childless women: Daniel Martin, 'Barren Britain: 19% of Women Are Childless at Menopause', *The Daily Mail* (19 May 2011); 'I've Come to My Senses over Delayed Motherhood', *The Daily Mail* (12 July 2006); Kate Mulvey, 'Duped Out of Motherhood', *The Daily Mail* (24 February 2006); 'Late Motherhood "Raises Breast Cancer Risk"', *The Daily Mail* (12 February 2002); 'Career Women's Bay Hunger', *The Daily Mail* (27 June 2003); Richard Ford, 'Fifth of Women Childless as Careers Take Precedence, Study Shows', *The Times* (26 June 2009); Press Association, 'Pressure of Work and Motherhood Pushed Woman to Suicide, Inquest Hears', *The Guardian* (28 July 2009); Yvonne Roberts, 'High-fliers Still "Marginalised by Motherhood"', *The Guardian* (21 November 2004); Lucy Caven-dish, 'Motherhood: Stay-at-home or back-to-work? The Battle Continues', *The Guardian* (28 March 2010); Jessica Shepherd, 'Girls Should Be "Realistic" about Careers and Motherhood—Schools Group Head', *The Guardian* (13 November 2009); Lizzy Davies,

recycled from the late nineteenth century took on a new, positive message of empowerment for the postfeminist target consumer—claiming that women could achieve the upper hand in gender relations through a potent coupling of consumerism and (hetero)sexuality—the reality of young women's situations was that they were the most likely victims of the things that popular culture suggested were their greatest weapons: money and sex. Far from being autonomous in either area, young women in fin-de-siècle twentieth-century Western society found themselves the new faces of AIDS and bankruptcy.

'French Philosopher Says Feminism Under Threat from "Good Motherhood"', *The Guardian* (12 February 2010); Daniel Bates, 'We're Tired all the Time, Say 60 Percent of Working Mothers', *The Daily Mail* (27 September 2007); Heather Weathers, 'Why Does Britain Have Record Levels of Abortion and an Unprecedented Need for IVF?', *The Daily Mail* (30 June 2006); Fiona Macrae, 'Women Who Give Birth over the Age of 30 Double their Risk of Breast Cancer', *The Daily Mail* (20 April 2007); Fiona Macrae, 'Women Have Just an Eighth of their Eggs Left by 30, Scientists Warn', *The Daily Mail* (27 January 2010); Melanie Phillips, 'Heading for Extinction?', *The Daily Mail* (22 June 2005); Carol Sarler, 'Why Bosses Are Right to Distrust Women Who Don't Want Children...by a VERY Outspoken Mother (and Ex-boss)', *The Daily Mail* (21 May 2009); Jeremy Laurance, 'Late Motherhood: Why Babies Can't Wait', *The Independent* (15 January 2008); Sophie Goodchild and Francis Elliot, 'Fertility Trap: The £500,000 Question—Should You Gamble with Your Body Clock?', *The Independent* (19 February 2006); Jeremy Laurance, 'Doctors Issue Health Warning on Women Who Give Birth Late', *The Independent* (16 September 2006); Maxine Frith, 'IVF Success Stories Are "Misleading"', *The Independent* (20 October 2005); Jeremy Laurance, 'The Baby Clock: Birth Survey Has Reignited Debate on Delayed Motherhood', *The Independent* (28 November 2008); Haroon Siddique, 'Delayed Motherhood behind Increase in Down's Syndrome Babies, Research Says', *The Guardian* (27 October 2009); Denis Campbell, 'Doctors Warn of Risks to Older Mothers', *The Guardian* (15 June 2009); Sarah Hall, 'Having Babies Boosts Women's Chances of Longer, Healthier Life', *The Guardian* (12 September 2006); Gaby Hinsliff and Lorna Martin, 'How the Baby Shortage Threatens our Future', *The Guardian* (19 February 2006); Tim Radford, 'EU Faces Big Drop in Birth Rate', *The Guardian* (28 March 2003); Deborah Orr, 'Is Feminism Really Killing the Family?', *The Guardian* (3 December 2009); 'A Breeding Liberty', *The Guardian* (20 September 1999); Madelaine Bunting, 'Baby, This Just Isn't Working for Me: Sidelined, Overlooked, Squeezed Out...The Mothers of Young Children Are More Discriminated against than Anyone Else in the Workplace, according to a New Report', *The Guardian* (1 March 2007); Ann Dally, *Inventing Motherhood: The Consequences of an Ideal* (New York: Schocken Books, 1985); Claudia Wallis, 'The Case for Staying at Home', *Time* (22 March 2004), pp. 50-59; Judith Warner, 'The Myth of the Perfect Mother: Why it Drives Real Women Crazy', *Newsweek* (21 February 2005), pp. 42-49; Anne Crittendon, *The Price of Motherhood: Why the Most Important Job in the World Is Still the Least Valued* (New York: Owl Books, 2002); Susan J. Douglas and Meredith W. Michaels, *The Mommy Myth: The Idealization of Motherhood and How it Has Undermined All Women* (New York: Free Press, 2004); Rebecca Asher, *Shattered: Modern Motherhood and the Illusion of Equality* (New York: Harvill Secker, 2011).

The situation in which today's young women find themselves problematizes postfeminist advertising. In the twentieth and twenty-first centuries there has been a sharp rise in the numbers of young women infected with the AIDS virus because public health information was, and is, directed at gay men, traditionally considered the 'high-risk' group. The sexual risk being taken by young people of all sexual persuasions has been virtually ignored until recently.

The nineteenth and twentieth century fin-de-siècles were characterized by similar apocalyptic social fears, with epidemics of deadly sexual infection, worries of urban decay and social degeneration and the threat of the 'New Woman' looming large. Indeed, the New Woman seems to be blamed for many of society's ills, which were often seen as punishment for improper sexual behaviour. The New Woman posed a threat to the stability of the traditional family unit, the breakdown of this family unit being cited as a major contributing factor towards the spread of AIDS and syphilis. Elaine Showalter draws parallels between the two fin-de-siècle sexual epidemics in her chapter 'The Way We Write Now: Syphilis and AIDS':[7]

> Both diseases have provided the occasion for sexual and social purity campaigns and for a retreat from the liberalization of sexual attitudes. Viewing syphilis as divine retribution for the collapse of sexual and marital boundaries, doctors in the 1890s began to publicize the dangers of an epidemic... Syphilis became an obsessive public crisis at the precise moment when arguments over the future of marriage, discussions of the New Woman, and decadent homosexual culture were at their peak. Conservatives were quick to seize upon the disease as a weapon in their fight to restore the values of chastity and monogamy; 'continence...became the hallmark of all sexual prescription'.[8]

The anxieties over these diseases are symbolized in visual culture, with Eve acting as a representation of sexual transgression and a reminder of the consequences of stepping outside of traditional gender roles. Eve acted in an autonomous manner in Genesis 3 when she discussed the possibility of eating the fruit with the serpent, but her autonomy brought about the expulsion of humankind from the Garden of Eden. In the nineteenth century, when gender upheaval and sexual epidemic were at a crisis point, Eve offered a visual cautionary tale against allowing women independence. Just as Eve brought death and suffering to the world so women in the nineteenth century were blamed for social breakdown and the spread of disease.

---

7.   Elaine Showalter, 'The Way We Write Now: Syphilis and AIDS', in her *Sexual Anarchy*, pp. 188-208.
8.   Showalter, 'The Way We Write Now', p. 188.

It is no longer the case that Eve offers a visual cautionary tale. Now, at the fin-de-siècle and in the twenty-first, century images of Eve's transgressive behaviour are being celebrated in advertising as 'feminine power', and female consumers are encouraged to enjoy the fruits of their financial and sexual independence. Ironically, the realities of contemporary young women's economic and sexual health, while they are being simply overlooked by the government, are completely ignored by advertisers for obvious reasons—it is difficult to sell insolvency and infection. Where advertising ignored the problem the media was not much better. If it did give attention to these problems it focused on the so-called 'high-risk' groups, particularly male homosexuals, as part of an ideologically charged push for a return to traditionally defined gender roles and monogamous heterosexuality.[9] The image of Eve, which shows the sexually assertive and confident young woman, aware and in control of her sexuality, is in sharp contrast to the findings of sociologists and medical doctors such as Janet Holland and others, whose groundbreaking research paper, 'Sex, Gender and Power: Young Women's Sexuality in the Shadow of AIDS', paints a bleaker picture:[10]

> The social pressures and constraints through which young women negotiate their sexual encounters impinge directly on their ability to make decisions about sexual safety and pleasure. The power of young women to control sexual practices can then play a key role in the transmission or limitation of sexually transmitted diseases. From preliminary analysis of data collected by the Women, Risk and AIDS Project, we argue that the risks young women take in sexual encounters with men arise within a nexus of contradictions through which women are expected to negotiate safer sex practices. However well intentioned, public health campaigns aimed at women cannot be effective unless they recognize that men and women begin their sexual encounters as unequal partners in the battle against the sexual transmission of HIV.[11]

9.   This 'moral panic' in itself reflects that of the nineteenth-century fin-de-siècle, as Showalter describes: 'As we live through our own age of venereal peril, the parallels between syphilis and AIDS seem particularly striking'. Elizabeth Fee notes that both diseases can be understood in terms as biomedical or moral: 'Both diseases can be transmitted by sexual contact; both can also be transmitted non-sexually. The social perception of each disease has been heavily influenced by the possibility of sexual transmission and the attendant notions of responsibility, guilt and blame. In each case, those suffering from the disease have often been regarded as both the cause and embodiment of the disease, and have been feared and blamed by others at the height of periods of anarchy, both syphilis and AIDS have been interpreted as the inevitable outcome of the violation of "natural" sexual laws' (Showalter, 'The Way We Write Now', pp. 189-90).
10.   Janet Holland *et al.*, 'Sex, Gender and Power: Young Women's Sexuality in the Shadow of AIDS', *Sociology of Health and Illness* 12.3 (1990), pp. 336-50.
11.   Holland *et al.*, 'Sex, Gender and Power', p. 336.

Unlike the media messages being marketed to young women in news-papers and advertising through the postfeminist Eve images, Janet Holland and her colleagues found that, with very few exceptions, young women 'lack a positive sense of their own sexual identity'.[12] Although Holland's article was written in 1990, little has changed in the twenty years since. In August 2010 The UK's Health Protection Agency[13] published a report on young people and sexually transmitted diseases. The report's press release headline stated 'Young Women Most at Risk',[14] and the report's findings were widely disseminated in the national press,[15] including the quote from Dr Gwenda Hughes, Head of the HPA's STI section, which echoes the findings of Holland *et al.*, decades previously: 'These figures also highlight the vulnerability of young women. Many studies have shown that young adults are more likely to have unsafe sex and often they lack the skills and confidence to negotiate safer sex'.[16] In 2008 the Centers for Disease Control and Prevention[17] reported similar findings in the US, '"High S.T.D. infection rates among young women, particularly young African-American women, are clear signs that we must continue developing ways to reach those most at risk," said Dr. John M. Douglas Jr., who directs the centers' division of S.T.D. prevention'.[18]

12.   Holland *et al.*, 'Sex, Gender and Power', p. 340.

13.   The Health Protection Agency 'is an independent UK organisation that was set up by the government in 2003 to protect the public from threats to their health from infectious diseases and environmental hazards. It does this by providing advice and information to the general public, to health professionals such as doctors and nurses, and to national and local government.' From The Health Protection Agency Website, http://www.hpa.org.uk/AboutTheHPA/ (accessed 25 August 2011).

14.   See the HPA report press release at http://www.hpa.org.uk/web/HPAweb& HPAwebStandard/HPAweb_C/1281953109509 (accessed 25 August 2011).

15.   For example, Sophie Borland, 'Teenage Girls Most at Risk as STIs in the UK Reach Record Levels', *The Guardian* (25 August 2010); Jane Dreaper, 'Sexually Trans-mitted Infections Near 0.5m a Year in UK', *BBC Health* (25 August 2010); Sarah Boseley, 'Young at Risk as Sexually Transmitted Infections Reach Record Levels: Peak Age for a Sexually Transmitted Infection is 19–20 for Women and 20–23 for Men, says Health Protection Agency', *The Guardian* (25 August 2010); Rebecca Smith, 'Sexually Transmitted Infections at Record High', *The Telegraph* (25 August 2010).

16.   Health Protection Agency Press Release, 'Sexually Transmitted Infections Reach Almost Half a Million' (25 August 2010), http://www.hpa.org.uk/web/HPAweb&HP AwebStandard/HPAweb_C/1281953109509 (accessed 25 August 2010).

17.   The Centers for Disease Control and Prevention is one of the 13 major operating components of the United States Department of Health and Human Services and a world authority on public health.

18.   Quotation from The Centers for Disease Control and Prevention news confer-ence, reported in Lawrence K. Altman, 'Sex Infections Found in a Quarter of Teenage Girls', *The New York Times* (12 March 2008).

Similarly, the 2012 Women's Research Initiative on HIV/AIDS reported that

> Risk factors affecting women's acquisition of HIV can be societal, structural, individual or, more likely, some combination of the three. They are extremely diverse and variable, and can include such issues as lack of female controlled prevention methods, high rates of sexual and gender-based violence, prevalence of heterosexual anal sex, concurrent sex partnerships, other sexually transmitted diseases, lack of access to information and healthcare, poverty, high-risk partnerships with men (history of incarceration, intravenous drug use, etc.), provider bias about HIV risk and social and cultural pressure to bear children, appease partners and demonstrate loyalty through trust.[19]

The reality of the unequal power dynamics in young women's sexual relationships is being ignored by advertisers in favour of a more attractive, lucrative option. Although young women are being offered images of heterosexual relations as the way in which they can achieve power, influence and independence in society, in fact they experience an imbalance in power in sexual negotiations, resulting in their inability to control the practice of safer sex in their relationships.[20] Consider this image of Eve, taken from the Fall 2010 ad campaign series for the handbag manufacturer Chenson (Fig. 2.0):

Figure 2.0. *Print advertisement for Chenson Handbags, 2010*

19. Women's Initiative on HIV/AIDS, 2012 Meeting Summary, http://www. thewellproject.org/en_US/About_Us/WRI_2012_Summary_Report.pdf (accessed 13 April 2012).

20. J. Jones, 'Young Women and Sexual Health', *National AIDS Bulletin/Australian Federation of AIDS Organisations Inc.* 5.6 (July 1991), pp. 18-20.

This image is typical of the type of advertising that young women are confronted with regularly in magazines and on billboards. Eve, the epitome of contemporary ideals in beauty, stares directly at the viewer, one hand holding the fruit and the other over her head in a posture of confident self-display. There are no worries about sexual infection here. It is unsurprising that the target consumer for this advertisement is suffering from the 'lack of positive self-identity' reported by Holland. *Glamour* magazine has a target female reader aged 17–25, meaning that the viewer of this image, although implied to be male, will be a young female consumer. She must identify with both Eve and the male viewer, effectively seeing herself through male eyes. The assertive Eve here knows she is attractive, enjoys the fact that she is attractive, and uses it for her gain, a picture that is in stark contrast to the reality of young women's sexual experiences and sense of self-confidence.

Of course, advertisers want to sell fantasy not reality. They would not need to sell the idea of sexual power to women if women were already experiencing that power. Advertising must sell concepts and qualities that are desirable to the consumer; the consumer must want to embody those concepts and qualities to buy the product. Therefore, the image of Eve the sexually autonomous temptress is merely reflecting what young women might like to be, according to the market research of the advertising companies, rather than who they are in the contemporary world.

> There is certainly evidence from our interviews that young women can be very active in resisting men's power, but their resistance may not necessarily be effective. It is clear from our respondents' accounts that young women are actively engaged in constructing their femininity and sexuality, but it is also clear that the negotiation of sexual encounters is a contradictory process in which young women generally lack power.[21]

The findings of Holland and others are far from the suggestions of prevalent Eve images, such as Figure 2.1, in which Eve appears be the dominant sexual partner. In this image, an underwear advert from the Spanish edition of *Vogue*, the fact that Eve is clothed in contrast to the posse of near-naked Adams surrounding her suggests that she enjoys a higher status than the men. Furthermore, the fact that the postures of the men mimic those of the traditionally female sex object (with Eve positioned in the centre, one of the men at her feet) indicates that the sexual power dynamics are in her favour. A postfeminist woman's first reading of this image would be that Eve has not only reached equal status to men but has gone beyond it.

21.   Holland *et al.*, 'Sex, Gender and Power', p. 341.

Figure 2.1. *Print advertisement for Duloren underwear, 1999*

In fact, attitudes to female sexuality appear not have progressed greatly in the hundred years since the nineteenth-century fin-de-siècle, as 'sexually active women are in constant danger of having negative identities attributed to them'.[22] Holland and her co-writers again found that 'women who challenge male definitions by revealing their own needs and desires for sex have negative images as rapacious and devouring, or as sluts':[23]

> Women who seek their own sexual pleasure with different partners were seen by some of our informants as 'slags' or as 'doing what lads do'. Others saw sex primarily as what you do to keep your boyfriend happy or, more negatively, what you do to keep him. It is difficult for young women to insist on safe sexual practices, when they do not expect to assert their own needs in sexual encounters.[24]

Indeed, according to a 2010 survey by The Havens (Sexual Assault Referral Centres) female victims of sexual assault are still subject to a culture of blame,[25] findings confirmed by Amnesty International's Stop Violence Against Women Campaign surveys and public reactions to the 2012 jailing of Sheffield United player, Ched Evans, for rape. Almost immediately following Evans's sentencing in April 2012 supporters of Evans took to Social Media site Twitter to set up #justiceforched and

22.   S. Lees, *Losing Out: Sexuality and Adolescent Girls* (London: Hutchinson, 1986).

23.   Holland *et al.*, 'Sex, Gender and Power', p. 340.

24.   J. Holland, C. Ramazanoglu and S. Scott, 'AIDS: From Panic Stations to Power Relations', *Sociology* 24.3 (1990), pp. 499-518.

25.   Opinion Matters, 'Wake Up to Rape Research Summary Report', *The Havens* (Sexual Assault Referral Centres, February 2010), http://www.thehavens.co.uk/docs/Havens_Wake_Up_To_Rape_Report_Summary.pdf (accessed February 2010).

#chedevans hashtags to show support for the convicted rapist and to
direct abusive comments at the victim of the rape, including calling her a
'slag'. Levels of abuse directed at the victim increased throughout the
day. *The Guardian* reported that 'Rape culture, which includes victim
blaming, sexual objectification and trivialising rape, was demonstrably
alive and well on both hashtags, and continued all weekend',[26] and ended
its article on the Twitter response to Evans's conviction with 'While it
may be without doubt that those who used Twitter in an unlawful way
over this issue should be punished, and it is fair to say that the law is
constantly being tested in its application in our new media age, what this
weekend has demonstrated is how alarmingly alive and pervasive rape
culture is. Isn't the biggest question what we do about that?'[27]

Temptresses get it all in advertising and Eve is the ultimate icon to
sell a new image of themselves to women, but one of the major socio-
economic issues in contemporary society shows the fallacy of the postfeminist Eve image, however. Far from achieving high social status and
financial independence through the consumption of products, young
women are more likely to suffer serious financial problems.

The cost of trying to appear financially successful and sexually attractive is proving to be more than young women can afford. The US,[28] UK[29]

26.   Amanda Bancroft, 'Twitter Reaction to Ched Evans Case Shows Rape Culture Is
Alive and Kicking: Some Tweets Directed at the Woman Raped by Evans May Be
Punishable, but the Attitudes that Led to them Need Tackling', *The Guardian* (23 April
2012).
27.   Bancroft, 'Twitter Reaction'.
28.   See Anya Kamenetez, *Generation Debt: Why Now Is a Terrible Time to Be Young*
(New York: Riverhead Books, 2006); Robert D. Manning, *Credit Card Nation: The
Consequences of America's Addiction to Credit* (New York: Basic Books, 2002); Liz Perle,
Money, a Memoir: Women, Emotions and Cash (New York: Henry Holt & Co., 2006);
Tamara Draut, *Strapped: Why America's 20 and 30 Somethings Can't Get Ahead* (New
York: Anchor Books, 2005); John De Graf *et al.*, *Affluenza: The All Consuming Epidemic*
(San Francisco: Berret-Koehler Publishers, 2005); James D. Scurlock, *Maxed Out: Hard
Times, Easy Credit* (London: HarperCollins, 2007); Teresa A. Sullivan *et al.*, *As We
Forgive our Debtors: Bankruptcy and Consumer Credit in America* (Washington, DC: Beard
Books, 1999); Oliver James, *Affluenza* (London: Vermilion, 2007) and the New York
Policy Group, DEMOS, briefing Paper, 'Generation Broke: The Growth of Debt among
Young Americans', 2005, for studies into the US economic difficulties for young people.
29.   The news headlines during most of the first decade of the twenty-first century
have included something about the sharp rise in bankruptcy and IVAs for young adults,
especially women; however, the 'epidemic' has been brewing for years: See Huma
Qureshi, 'Young Women Overtake Men in Bankruptcy Stakes', *The Guardian* (17 June
2009); Rachel Shields, 'Debt Is a Feminist Issue: Huge Leap in Bankruptcy among
Women', *The Independent* (25 July 2010); Melissa Kite, 'Female Bankrupts: Girls Lose

and Australia[30] are all seeing dramatic rises in the insolvency of young adult females, to the point where the trend is being called an epidemic.[31] The rise in personal bankruptcies and IVAs[32] among women is due to 'irresponsible spending'[33] according to the director of Wilkins Kennedy Accountants, Anthony Cork. Cork concludes that young women's current financial distress is due to several factors. One is the dual pressures of striving to maintain a consumer lifestyle while looking attractive:

> Five years ago, it tended to be young men who got out of their financial depth, but now it is far more likely to be young women who spend irresponsibly. Over the last decade the pressure on young women to follow the lavish lifestyle of female celebrities has grown immensely. The growing availability of credit has meant that for those status-conscious, who want to exhibit the trappings of success, designer clothes and jewellery seem misleadingly achievable.[34]

Another is that pursuing independent, single lives is expensive:

> Too many young single women have taken out mortgages that eat up far too much of their monthly salaries. This makes them vulnerable to changes in interest rates and makes them far more likely to go bankrupt if they lose their job.[35]

the Blues in the Red', *The Telegraph* (20 June 2009); Alastair Jamieson, 'Young Women "Lured into Bankruptcy by Celebrity Lifestyle"', *The Telegraph* (17 June 2009); Olina Koster, 'Young, Female and Bankrupt: Lure of a Celebrity Lifestyle Leads to Rise in Women Going Bust', *The Daily Mail* (17 June 2009); Louise Brittain, 'Sisters Are Doing it to Themselves as Female Bankruptcies Rise', Web News Release from the top ten accountancy firm Baker Tilly, Thursday 28 June 2001; Helen Nugent, 'Bankrupt Women Paying for Credit Cards', *Times Online* (16 May 2005) (http://business.timesonline.co.uk); Sean Poulter and Becky Barrow, 'Middle-class Debts Soar in Quest for Designer Lifestyle', *The Daily Mail* (24 May 2006); Lech Mintowt-Czyz, 'Bankrupt Women Pay the Price of High Living', *The Daily Mail* (27 July 2001); Laurie Osborne, 'Britain's Bankrupt P.Y.T.s', *The Guardian* (16 June 2005); BBC Radio 4's *Woman's Hour* programme, 'The Impact of Borrowing and Debt on Women's Lives' (14 June 2005).

30. Louise Brogan, 'Going for Broke', *Sydney Morning Herald* (11 November 2001), and David Koch, 'Shocking Debt Ruins Young Women's Debut', *Sydney Morning Herald* (23 April 2006).

31. Louise Brittain, a bankruptcy specialist and partner at the top ten accountancy firm Baker Tilly estimated in 2001 that female bankruptcies were growing at a rate of 20–25% annually from *News Release* (28 June 2001).

32. An IVA is an Individual Voluntary Arrangement, a legally binding agreement with creditors that allows the debtor to pay a sum of money to them for between three to five years to avoid bankruptcy.

33. Sean Poulter, 'Debt Piles Up for Young Women', *The Daily Mail* (14 November 2005).

34. Qureshi, 'Young Women Overtake Men in Bankruptcy Stakes'.

35. Quershi, 'Young Women Overtake Men in Bankruptcy Stakes'.

The UK Insolvency Service, who collates the figures, reported that it was women's 'typically low monthly salaries' that were the real cause of female insolvency. Indeed, Cork's comments seem inaccurate, however, given that similar headlines claiming that women are falling into a trap of celebrity-lifestyle-induced debt have been reported annually for the past decade. For example, in 2005 Debt Management Company, ClearDebt, reported almost identical comments to those of Cork in relation to that year's insolvency figures:

> We see a lot of young women with three, four and five credit cards which are spent up to their limit on clothes and holidays. Young women are under greater pressure than men to spend more of their money on looking good, fashions and going out. But the evidence is that many are simply living ahead of their income... There is evidence that young women are striking out on their own, pursuing their independence and setting up home, much more readily than men. However, this generates its own debts in terms of finding the money to pay rents, mortgages, bills and living expenses.[36]

And in 2004, Patrick Boyden, a partner at PriceWaterhouseCoopers, a consumer trend analysis firm, that found that forty-five percent more women went bankrupt in 2003/4 than the previous year, and confirmed the statistics, saying, 'A new bankrupt is emerging who is more likely to be female, under thirty and has not been in business before'.[37]

This surge in insolvency among young women should be unexpected, given the 'financial autonomy' and consumer power that they are supposed to be wielding in the late twentieth/early twenty-first century, but the problem is that they do not really have the financial means to gratify the consumeristic desires inculcated in them by advertisers. Women's income is still thirteen percent lower than a man's for an equivalent job, and lack of real progression in childcare provision means that women still have to shoulder the financial responsibility for parenting, with twenty percent of women facing dismissal or wage loss because of pregnancy.[38] Despite recent proposals by the government, pensions are still designed for people who work full-time all of their working lives, leaving women (still overwhelmingly the main care-givers for children) financially short-changed. Nevertheless, young women's debt levels are rising in spite of their static income because, as Keith Stevens, a partner at PricewaterhouseCoopers, states, 'The root of the problem is that women have seen the rapid growth in their financial independence outstrip the

36. Andrew Smith from ClearDebt quoted in Nugent, 'Bankrupt Women Paying for Credit Cards', *Times Online* (16 May 2005) (http://business.timesonline.co.uk).
37. Quotation from Keith Stevens in Poulter, 'Debt Piles Up for Young Women'.
38. Crittendon, *The Price of Motherhood*.

rise in their incomes'.[39] Similarly, Helen Nugent of *The Times* observes, 'a combination of women's growing financial independence and the fact that they continue to earn less than men means that forty-two percent of bankrupts are female'.[40]

If women are earning less than men, lose job security and savings through maternity[41] and face the glass ceiling in terms of job prospects,[42] what exactly is the 'financial independence' that the financial experts speak of? Women are no longer entirely dependent on men and marriage to support them,[43] but women who support themselves often take on far more financial risk than their income allows. This 'independence' comes in the form of credit. The 'consumer power' of the postfeminist ideology is actually the ability to spend borrowed money, which young women then find themselves unable to repay. The consumer group *Which?* has blamed the 'slick marketing material',[44] targeting young women specifically, for the rise in female bankruptcies: 'Women are particularly susceptible to companies' tactics of teasing customers into certain spending patterns. They want people to spend money today and pay it off another time.'[45] Women are taking up the offer of a 'buy now, pay later' culture

39. Patrick Boyden, quoted in Poulter, 'Debt Piles Up for Young Women'.

40. Nugent, 'Bankrupt Women Paying for Credit Cards'. The figure of 42% for the proportion of women bankrupts is currently higher—in the same period of 2006, 50% of bankrupts were women, a massive increase on even five years previously (the number of women bankrupts rose by one third from 2000 to 2005 according to *The Times* [16 May 2005]).

41. In her 2002 bestselling polemic, *The Price of Motherhood*, Ann Crittenden claims that rearing children will cost a college-educated woman nearly a million dollars in lifetime earnings, and that motherhood is still the single best predictor of poverty in women.

42. In the US in 2004, women held only a 13.6% proportion of board seats at the nation's 500 largest companies (source: Anya Kamenetez, 'Generation Debt: Superwoman 2.0—Your Biological Clock. Your Student Loans. Your Girly Paycheck. Hey, You're Having it All', *News: Village Voice* (21 December 2004) (http://www.villagevoice.com [accessed 21 December 2004]).

43. Of the dozens of women on the 2004 *Forbes* Richest People list, nearly all of them made their fortunes through marriage.

44. Quotation from Laurence Baxter, Senior policy advisor at *Which?* in *The Times* (16 May 2005). Also, research from a 2003 survey by the Dieringer Research Group found that women were more likely than men to research and be influenced by Internet advertising for credit cards and other financial products, stating, 'If you're not targeting Gen X/Y women online for your financial/insurance products—or for many other product categories—you're probably missing an important market growth opportunity'. Quotation in Janet Kidd Stewart, 'Generation IOU: Credit Card Debt and College Loans Are Creating Financial Hardship for Many of Today's Young Working Women', *The Chicago Tribune* (27 April 2005). Comments like this reinforce another stereotype: like Eve, women are fallible, easily persuaded (unlike men presumably).

45. Kidd Stewart, 'Generation IOU'.

created by credit card companies, and analysts agree that young women
are spending their borrowed money on 'a high-octane lifestyle of socialis-
ing and spending on luxury goods'[46] and 'designer clothes and extravagant
social lives'.[47] Yet, both the Fawcett Society and the TUC[48] have found
that far from being the serial profligate spender construct of the media
reports, female poverty is not caused by aspirations to emulate Victoria
Beckham but because women in the UK are still paid approximately
14.9% less than men for the equivalent job; are still more likely to
experience gender discrimination in the work-place; and the UK continues to have unequal child-caring roles for women and men so that
women are more likely to be employed in low paid, part-time work. For
example, according the Fawcett Society, in 2010 one in five women were
living in poverty, while nine out of ten lone parents are women and the
median gross weekly pay for male single parents is £346, while for female
single parents it is £194.40. There is, it seems, a world of difference
between the bankrupt Paris Hilton wannabes of the newspaper columns
and the real face of female poverty.[49]

Figure 2.2. *Print advertisement for El Palacio de Hierro Department Store, 2004*

Advertising helps to construct and perpetuate the irresponsible female
spender stereotype so beloved of the media. Eve is an advertiser's 'dream
girl' for selling luxury goods. Her image has been used to sell cars,

46. Michael Clarke, 'Young Women Fuel Bankruptcy Rise', *This Is Money* (10 June
2005) (http://www.thisismoney.co.uk/credit-and-loans/debt-news/article.html).
47. Mintowt-Czyz, 'Bankrupt Women Pay the Price of High Living'.
48. 'TUC, Women and Recession: How Will this Recession Affect Women at
Work?' (January 2009) (http://www.tuc.org.uk/extras/womenandrecession.pdf [accessed
12 January 2009]).
49. The Fawcett Society Equal Pay 2010 Campaign Report, http://www.
fawcettsociety.org.uk/index.asp?PageID=321 (3 April 2010).

designer clothes and an overall luxury lifestyle that is marketed as being normal for the average young woman. The ad above (Fig. 2.2) promotes the luxury department store El Palacio de Hierro in Mexico. In the image Eve's pre-bitten forbidden fruit is substituted for a shoe, signifying the stereotype of the shoe-obsessed female shopper. In this ad Eve knows she should not buy any more shoes but she does so regardless of the (financial) consequences.

In Australia, the manager of Sydney's Creditline Financial Services, Richard Brading, blames media targeting of young women in advertising campaigns for the sudden growth of female insolvents there,[50] stating that, 'It's our lifestyle, young women are subjected to an enormous barrage of advertisements for expensive products, high fashion, cosmetics, and they're spending more than they can afford on credit cards simply to keep up with their peers. They'll shop to boost self-confidence and deal with emotions.'[51]

Another Eve-related ad for El Palacio de Hierro department store (Fig. 2.3) shows how the constant visibility of women and the judgment of them based on that visibility necessitates the constant updating of the wardrobe. As the ad says 'The problem is not how good or bad it fits. But that everybody has already seen it.'

Figure 2.3. *Print advertisement for El Palacio del Hierro Department Store, 2004*

50.   According to Reserve Bank Figures, in July 2001 Australia's credit card debt was $18.6 billion, triple the amount for the same month in 1995.

51.   Quotation from Richard Brading in Louise Brogan, 'Going for Broke: The Latest Hairstyles, Shoes, Designer Outfit and Restaurant Are a Seductive Lure to Many Young Women Who Are Plunging Themselves into Debt to Maintain the High Life', *The Sydney Morning Herald* (11 November 2001).

Both Richard Brading and policy coordinator, Sharon Baker, at the Financial and Consumer Rights Council in Victoria, Australia, believe that young women are susceptible to borrowing, and overspending, money because of deeply embedded self-esteem issues:

> Easy credit is only part of the problem, the other issue is that many young women see spending as a validation of their worth. It's about image, about the media, look at women's magazines these days—it's not difficult understand why young women feel compelled to go out and spend a lot of money on clothing and make-up when the media clearly indicates that that's what you've got to do to be considered a member of society.[52]

It may not be just a matter of low self-esteem for these many insolvent young women across Western society—although the research into the power imbalances in young women's sexual relationships seems to support the conclusion that they are suffering from a general disempowerment in contemporary society—but also a poorly thought-out political move. In postfeminist culture, the representation of identity is a political process capable of reinforcing power relations in society. If women are in control of representing themselves after a history of being represented by men, as in the nineteenth-century fin-de-siècle *femme fatale* images, then how they portray themselves, both personally and in the media, is indicative of their status in contemporary society. Women who overspend on luxury goods in an attempt to create the impression that their social standing is higher than it really is are merely following the example of popular culture, which creates the illusion that women wield more power than they hold in reality. The power associated with the images of Eve employed in contemporary advertising is the ability to attract the men. This attraction somehow allows women, or attractive women at least, to gain more influence, status and economic power than would otherwise be the case. The 'power' that advertisements suggest is ambiguous, however, since the viewer is not able to see the effects of Eve's power. She harnesses the male gaze, but does this make her a CEO of a top 100 PLC Company? Does it allow her to earn the same pay as the man who is looking at her? The power of Eve in advertising seems to be merely the traditional power of women to attract a mate rather than female autonomy.

While Eve ads are supposed to represent the new woman, they have in reality simply rehashed old, misogynistic images. Even in the context of a new postfeminist ideology where women are equal and even sexually dominant, these images still view women as sex objects whose worth and social status lie in their ability to be sexually attractive.

52.   Quotation in Brogan, 'Going for Broke'.

Although the naked female body has long been presented as a symbol of sexual lust in culture,[53] the fashion for depicting the woman as the locus of social evil reached its zenith in the nineteenth century at the fin-de-siècle, when the *femme fatale* genre of art became a cultural phenomenon. Artists such as Dante Gabriel Rossetti, Edward Burne-Jones, Gustave Moreau and Jean Delville produced images of macabre and maleficent female sexuality that, although produced by male artists for male viewers, were, like the Eve images in contemporary advertising, popular with both females and males at the time. Naturally, Eve, being synonymous with 'woman', was a favourite for representation; her cultural *doxa* embodied the essential qualities of a *femme fatale*—potent female sexuality and the destruction of the male—in a well-known biblical character. Biblical and mythical female characters proved popular with artists not only because the characters were familiar to the viewer, but because, by exploiting well-established stories, the images of evil female sexuality seemed to be based on cultural 'truths' about gender roles and the dangers of transgressing prescribed sexual roles.

Images of usually naked, always sexually provocative women were a measure of the social climate. As Patrick Bade asserts:

> The phenomenon of the *femme fatale* was far more than the artificial creation of a small number of artists who had problems with their mothers and mistresses. These men sensed and expressed the underlying anxieties of the age, which resulted from profound social change. Before the women's movement had made women conscious of their subservience and given voice to their grievances, poets and artists had realized that male dominance, which had evolved since the beginning of civilization, was becoming increasingly precarious.[54]

Like Bade, Virginia Allen sees the images of the *femme fatale* as a reflection of nineteenth-century fin-de-siècle society's grievous concerns with the rise of feminism:

> But if one is to say they (the artists) were sexually disturbed, even neurotic, then one is forced to say that a major aspect of the culture of Europe was equally neurotic. If they created an image based on neurotic sexual fantasy, that fantasy was nearly universal in Europe. The 'icon' they made was so sought after and so cogent for their contemporaries that its label entered the language. And they shared their culture's values.[55]

---

53. See Miles, *Carnal Knowing*, p. 81.
54. Bade, *Femme Fatale*, p. 39.
55. Allen, *The Femme Fatale*, p. 190.

The proliferation of *femme fatale* images in the late nineteenth century coincided with the significant change in women's socio-political position. The issue of the right of women to vote had been raised in the British Parliament in 1867 and the Married Women's Property Act, which established minimum legal rights for a married woman, was passed in 1870. Some educational and professional opportunities began to open up for women but, although this feminist progression was significant, the cultural response was exaggerated—almost verging on hysterical, considering the extreme visions of the nature and threat of femininity that were produced by artists. After all, these changes in women's position benefited only a small minority of women at the time and any attempt at the female autonomy that 1890's society found so worrisome was decades away.

Eve, as an erotic icon in art, represented these social and sexual fears of the nineteenth century fin-de-siècle and consequently she accrued 'an enormously intensified erotic and lethal power'.[56] In art, images show that social and sexual degeneration stemmed from the sexual female and her bid for emancipation. The 'New Woman' that feminism had created, who campaigned for emancipation, resisted the traditional social gender roles of the time and insisted on the right to be financially autonomous instead of dependant on a husband, was very much something to be feared. In her study on Eve in art for this period Allen states, 'female self-assertion implies instant sexual threat'. Eve was a symbol of the dangers of female self-assertion and images of Eve served as a warning to retain the clear demarcation between gender roles for the social good.

The New Woman was not the only type of female to be threatening the traditional social order at the end of the nineteenth century, however; the Odd Woman was causing almost as much upset. The term was used to describe the steadily increasing surplus of unmarried women in England. These single women were considered to be masculinizing themselves by earning their own living rather than fulfilling their duty by becoming a mother. They were independent but incomplete: 'As women sought opportunities for self-development outside of marriage, medicine and science warned that such ambitions would lead to sickness, freakishness, sterility and racial degeneration'.[57] The Italian Symbolist painter Giovanni Segatini painted several versions of a work entitled *The Wicked Mothers* (Fig. 2.4) in response to these Odd Women, who delayed or refused motherhood. The painting is an interpretation of a passage in the

56. Allen, *The Femme Fatale*, p. 185.
57. Showalter, *Sexual Anarchy*, p. 39.

Indian poem *Pangiavahli*, which describes the punishment inflicted in women who deny their biological role as child-bearer.

Figure 2.4. The Wicked Mothers, *Giovanni Segantini, 1894*

Figure 2.5. Punishment for Lasciviousness (Punishment for Lust),
Giovanni Segantini, 1894

In the painting *The Wicked Mothers*, those women who refuse maternity are tormented by their unborn babies, illustrating the suffering to be endured by women who do not bear children.[58] A woman is suspended in

58.   Wendy Slatkin, 'Maternity and Sexuality in the 1890s', *Women's Art Journal* 1.1 (1980), pp. 13-19 (16).

the foreground. She is trapped in a barren, frozen landscape, by the branches of the dead tree, which has caught her hair. As if whipped, her body is bending, and at her bare breast is a dead baby. The painting functions as a warning to women who reject their biological destiny. *Wicked Mothers* was only one version of a series Segantini painted on the theme of the woman who rejects her traditional maternal role. In *Punishment for Lasciviousness* (Fig. 2.5)[59] the women are doomed to float, naked, in a coma-like state, in a deserted frozen landscape as a punishment for their dismissal of traditional social gender roles and choosing against motherhood.

The nineteenth-century fin-de-siècle Odd Woman, the single woman who chooses self-development over motherhood, is pivotal to the discussion of Eve images in contemporary advertising. Although most contemporary Eve images are borrowed, sometimes almost exactly, from the nineteenth-century *femme fatale* paintings, it is this 'Odd Woman' who is the precursor to the postfeminist consumer of fin-de-siècle twentieth century. The New Woman is a feminist and fights for her financial independence but remains married and still abides by the mainstay of gender demarcation: marriage; however, this New Woman becomes an Odd Women when she does away with the need for a husband altogether. She has her own income and employment and she shuns her traditional duty of motherhood. As the twentieth century draws to a close the Odd Woman is reborn as the Career Woman, but in the 1990s, after second-wave feminism has mutated into postfeminism, the financially and sexually independent woman is celebrated rather than denounced in popular culture. She is now a market sector and therefore a highly valuable consumer, she is to be courted by advertising campaigns and her wealth targeted and harnessed through commercial consumption. In this climate, Eve, the *femme fatale*, begins to appear again. By the late 1990s there is a proliferation of her images in popular culture and they are photographic copies of the artworks of the nineteenth century.

A painting of Lilith by John Collier in the late 1880s (Fig. 2.6) shows us Eve's alter-ego, the first disobedient wife of Adam who was replaced by the more pliable Eve. By association she is Eve, and most viewers make the connection even without knowing the story of Lilith.[60] This image of the serpent-entwined woman connotes various concepts to the viewer: sin, dangerous female sexuality and temptation. In the nineteenth

59.   Also known as *Punishment for Lust*.
60.   Pamela Norris actually terms such representations as 'Lilith-Eve representations', since Eve is as much evoked as Lilith. See Norris, *The Story of Eve*, p. 10.

century she may have been the symbol of female maleficence but at the end of the twentieth century she is given a postfeminist makeover and she is now a symbol of the change in gender dynamics in contemporary society (Fig. 2.7).

 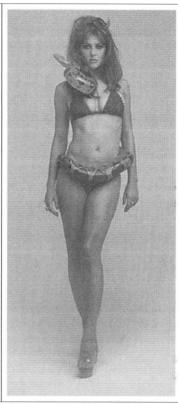

Figure 2.6. Lilith,
John Collier, 1887

Figure 2.7. *Online promotional
image for* Bedazzled, 2000

According to contemporary advertisements, women's ability to attract males is their most lucrative asset, and the images imply that the products that the advertisers are selling will either increase the potency of female sexuality or somehow imbue the consumer with female sexual power. For instance, Figure 2.7 shows Elizabeth Hurley promoting the 1999 film *Bedazzled*. She is in character as the Devil, the role she plays in the film. To advertise *Bedazzled*'s release Hurley posed for several promotional shots as sexy Satan, the modern retake on the nineteenth-century *femme fatale*. Hurley's career success has been founded on her physical beauty and this advertisement builds on the audience's knowledge of Hurley's persona. She poses in a bikini, with a serpent around her neck and horns have been added to her head to emphasize the Devil theme in the image. Hurley simultaneously links femininity with evil and the *femme fatale* image with the power to attract the gaze. Whereas the power of the nineteenth-century *femme fatale* was her ability to attract and destroy men, and usually themselves, as Segantini's paintings showed, the power of the twenty-first-century temptress Eve image is her ability to attract men to further her own ambitions. An example of Eve's function as a career 'booster' is most famously seen in an advertising campaign from the end of the twentieth century. Anthea Turner, the former highest paid female in television, found herself the victim of a severe media backlash in the late 1990s. Having constructed her public persona as a 'good girl' she fell foul of the tabloids when she had an affair with Grant Bovey, a married father of three. Turner went on to marry Bovey, but even their wedding day was marred with negative publicity when the newlyweds agreed to advertise a new chocolate bar, Cadbury Snowflake, in the wedding photos that were to be sold to celebrity interview magazine, *Hello*. Turner, in particular, was lambasted in the newspapers for the crassness of this move. Unfortunately, following her mauling in the media, Turner found herself a pariah of the early evening shows in which she had found such success. Her status had lurched from TV golden girl to unemployed 'has been' in the course of one year. When she attempted to exploit her new, media constructed, persona of temptress to increase her status, she posed for publicity shots as Eve.

Figure 2.8. *Promotional media image of*
Anthea Turner, The Sun, *17 March 1997*

The pose mirrors one of Franz von Stuck's many versions of his painting, *Sin* (Fig. 2.9).

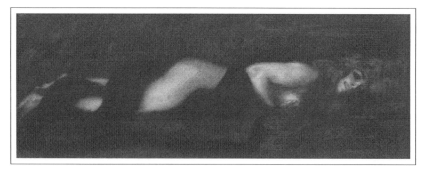

Figure 2.9. *Franz von Stuck, Sin, 1893*

Although the concepts communicated by the images are similar, the Von Stuck image is dark, deathly and sinisterly erotic. The image of Turner, however, does not have any of these undertones of sex and death; her photo is light, almost to the point of being clinical. She is not a true *femme fatale* in the nineteenth-century fin-de-siècle sense but is merely using this once again fashionable image to reverse the backlash she experienced and turn it to her advantage. In her photo Turner becomes not just a fallen former children's presenter who fell in love with a married man, but a woman of the times: she knows what she wants and she knows how to get it. She lies naked, in an all-white background, so that the focus of the image is on her body and the snake. Turner's posture is unnatural; she has raised her lower body to create a more prominent curve to her body, in an attempt to make the picture look more sexual. The serpent has been positioned to follow the emphasized curve of Turner's body, and she grasps the creature with both hands near her face to show closeness. To make the context of the image clear to the viewer, the snake faces a bright red apple, just in the left corner of the image. The apple matches the shade of Turner's lips, drawing a connection between Turner and the forbidden fruit. The fact that she has physical similarities to both the forbidden fruit and the serpent in the image implies that she also shares other qualities with them, such as being tempting and desirable. The serpent is carefully manipulated around her body so that it mirrors her own body's shape exactly, as if the woman and the snake are a visual echo of each other. Von Stuck's painting, however, seems to have the woman trapped within the dark coils of the snake. She does not look like she could get easily free of the serpent, but she is smiling, showing that she enjoys its grip. The postures and lighting of the two images suggest the difference in the socio-political climate of the cultures in which they were produced: Turner's light, airy shot, with the snake only next to her instead of wrapped around her suggests that she can easily be free of her association with the creature, whereas Von Stuck's image and the deathly pallor of the woman in the grip of the serpent suggests that she is trapped and has little chance of release. In other words, Turner as a twentieth-century woman chooses to play the role of the Eve to increase her status but the woman in Von Stuck's painting has little choice in her representation. She is ensnared in the role of maleficent seductress.

Turner's Eve is self-consciously postfeminist and almost a parody of her usual TV persona. She shows the audience that she is in on the joke by returning their gaze and smiling. The difficulty, Turner discovered, was that, for all the postfeminist propaganda and advertising ideology that currently saturates our culture, the sexual transgression of women remains unacceptable in Western society and Turner's career has never recovered from the press scandal of her affair despite her attempts to use Eve imagery to boost her flagging career. Modern women too, it seems, can be as trapped by gender roles as their nineteenth-century counterparts. Most likely for this very reason they can offer a fantasy image to which female consumers can aspire.

A print advertisement for *Trussardi Python* perfume (Fig. 2.10), another appropriation of the Eve image, shows a pose similar to the Turner promotional photograph, only this time all the hallmarks of postfeminist empowerment are absent. A naked woman stands in front of a white column that is similar in shape to the perfume bottle in the right-hand corner of the image. With one hand she holds on to the column and with the other she supports the enormous python that is coiled around her upper body. The naked woman stands in a traditionally feminine pose used in advertising, where the leg facing the camera is bent slightly to emphasize slenderness and length. Significantly, she pouts seductively and looks away from the camera, to something off scene.

In this image Eve is pictured in licensed withdrawal, which shows her removed psychologically from the situation depicted.[61] When Erving Goffman conducted his research in advertising in the 1970s he found that far more women than men were pictured in licensed withdrawal:

> Women more than men, it seems, are pictured engaged in involvements which remove them psychologically from the social situation at large, leaving them unoriented in it and to it, and presumably, therefore, dependent on the protectiveness and goodwill of others who (or might come to be) present.[62]

61. See Goffman, *Gender Advertisements*, p. 57.
62. Goffman, *Gender Advertisements*, p. 57.

Figure 2.10. *Print advertisement for* Trussardi Python for Women, 1999

As mentioned, above, and as I seek to illustrate further in what follows, in postfeminist Eve advertising the male character, Adam, is the one who is pictured in licensed withdrawal, leaving him disoriented and psychologically withdrawn from the scene. Eve, on the other hand, is usually pictured returning the viewers' gaze, as a sign of empowerment and sexual assertion. This is not always the case, however, as the Trussardi image illustrates.

Although the image seems to depict the woman as active in self-objectification, in reality it presents her as psychologically removed from the scenario. Because the woman is on display and in licensed withdrawal in the advertisement, she is not empowered by her objectification—she is not 'in' on the postfeminist joke. Instead, this image becomes just another sexually suggestive image of a naked woman with a phallic symbol hanging down her leg. All the traits of sexual empowerment that one would expect in postfeminist advertising are absent from this image: the traditional posture of feminine display rather than the assertive display posture of the postfeminist Eve, the absence of the active look of one who has agency in her objectification, and the absence of the forbidden fruit that has become the postfeminist symbol for individual choice and sexual empowerment are missing from this image of Eve. The bottle, the serpent and the column are all phallically shaped, suggesting that Eve is being objectified not only to attract men but for the pleasure of men.

Figure 2.11. *Print advertisement for Christian Dior Hypnotic Poison Perfume, 2009*

Figure 2.12. Sin, *Franz von Stuck, 1893*

An advertisement for Dior's *Hypnotic Poison* perfume bears a striking resemblance to another fin-de-siècle painting by Franz von Stuck (Figs. 2.11 and 2.12). Again, Von Stuck's snake-woman has no identity, she is in the shadows and her body, since it is the centre of sin, is made the focus of the painting and is centralized and highlighted. The woman's identity is her body, the viewer does not need to see her face; she needs no other identity than her sexuality. Dior's advertisement, featuring Monica Belluci, a French actress famous for her smouldering sexuality, once again brings Eve out into the light. Selling a luxury fragrance for a prestige brand, Belluci is evidence of the status a woman can achieve through beauty and sex appeal. Both women look back at the viewer but whereas Stuck's Eve appears ill, with her green-tinged complexion, Belluci's gaze is intended to have a 'hypnotic' effect on the viewer, she has the ability to make men do as she bids and she can teach female consumers to be the same—with just a small investment of cash.

3

Bad Girls Sell Well:
The Commodification of
Eve in Postfeminist Consumerism

That bad girl power I got, I'll abuse it tonight
Cause tonight got poison on my mind
That power I got, you'll be mine when I stay till real late
Got poison on my mind
I got that poison, I got that poison
I got that poison, that poison on my mind
I got that poison, that poison, that poison
I'll make you fall in love with me

—Nicole Scherzinger, *Poison* (2010)

You think I'm sexy, huh?
I'm international
Think you can make me fall?
What do you know?
I'm in my Louis Vuitton's,
Flyin' like a bomb,
And I'll be ducking calls 'til I go home

Girls bring the fun of life,
Sugar like apple pie,
Take a trip to paradise,
Let's have a party, y'all!
Beauty like you never saw,
Take your number, never call,
Bite the apple, take your heart,
Let's have a party, y'all!!

—Sugababes, *About a Girl* (2009)

She a bad girl, a real shopaholic,
She buying everything up man I can't call it,
And she a walking store, I'm talking 'bout her clothes,
I just pause, I'm in awe, cuz she a fashion show,
Real Louis bags and breathe Gucci,
Got a wardrobe like she's starring in a movie,

And she ain't even famous but she got her own groupies,
She got her own groupies,
She got her own groupies,
What a bad little girl I am (I got a problem)
What a bad little girl I am (I need you to solve it)
What a bad little girl I am
bad bad bad bad bad
—Rihanna (feat. Chris Brown), *Bad Girl* (2009)

Of the hundreds of advertisements I have examined in my extensive research on Eve imagery, the majority are of Eve alone, followed closely by images that show Adam and Eve together. In contrast, Adam appears alone in only about half a dozen advertisements.[1] This situation reflects the status of woman as sex object in popular culture and also the post-feminist social climate in which the images are produced. It also reflects the status of the woman in the biblical text. For me, as for popular culture and for so many interpreters over the centuries, Eve is the star of the story. So much narrative space is given to her in the so-called temptation scene in Gen. 3.1-7 that a visual depiction of this scene would tend to focus on Eve. In the biblical text Adam appears only at the end of the scene. Genesis 3 begins by introducing the serpent, who in v. 1 speaks to the woman. In vv. 2-5 the serpent and the woman discuss God's command not to eat the fruit of the tree, God's motive and the possible consequences of eating. In v. 6 the woman considers the possibilities: the tree is good for food, is pleasing to look at and is desirable to make one wise. So she takes some of its fruit and eats it. Up to this point there is no indication that the man is present, but the remainder of v. 6, 'and she also gave some to her husband who was with her and he ate', is crucial for a proper understanding of the biblical story, for it makes clear that both the man and the woman are present at the temptation scene and that the man raises no objections to the woman's decision to eat of the fruit. Her disobedience to God's command is active whereas his is passive.[2]

For centuries Eve has been blamed and condemned for leading Adam into temptation, and recent feminist biblical criticism has done little, if anything, to redeem her image outside the guild of biblical studies.[3] That

1. In the course of my research I have compiled a database of popular cultural images of Adam and Eve, in which 1027 of the images are of Eve and only 6 of them depict Adam alone.
2. Thus one of the consequences of their action is that the active sinner is made subordinate to the passive sinner (v. 16).
3. See, e.g., Trible, *God and the Rhetoric of Sexuality*, pp. 72-143; Kimelman, 'The Seduction of Eve and the Exegetical Politics of Gender'; Meyers, *Discovering Eve*, pp. 72-121; Phyllis A. Bird, *Missing Persons and Mistaken Identities: Women and Gender*

Eve is to be blamed for the so-called fall of humanity is, in my view, not
just a figment of the popular cultural imagination. She is blamed and
condemned in the text too. She is the one who consciously and actively
disobeys the divine command. She plays the stronger role. She is the first
to take the fruit and eat it. She *gave* the fruit to her husband who simply
eats. And, most damaging for Trible's argument that both the man and
the woman are equally guilty in transgression,[4] is Gen. 3.17, where God
says to the man, 'because *you obeyed your wife* and ate from the tree,
which I commanded you saying "you shall not eat of it", cursed is the
ground because of you; in toil you shall eat of it all the days of your life'.[5]
Indeed one would not expect an androcentric text produced by a patriarchal society to champion the cause of women. Even though the woman
in Gen. 3.1-6 has a stronger role, this text teaches a lesson about the
danger of allowing women to think for themselves and make decisions.
The consequences are disastrous, and thus convey to the reader the idea
that women should be subordinate to their husbands. Indeed, the subordination of the woman to the man is precisely the situation that Eve's
punishment achieves: 'your desire shall be for your husband, and he shall
rule over you'.

  Advertising makes explicit what is implicit in the text: Adam allowed
himself to be led astray by Eve. Thus women have power, the power to
lead men into temptation, as well as the power to make decisions for
themselves, regardless of the consequences. Where does this mysterious
female power lie? For advertisers the answer is in female sexuality, and
here one can argue that they are picking up on hints in the biblical text.
In advertisement Adam is a passive character who plays a minor role in
the temptation scene, just as he does in the text. Popular cultural interpretations frequently play on Adam's inability to resist his sexual desire
for Eve when she offers him the forbidden fruit.

  In advertising, offering the forbidden fruit, an apple, is a metaphor for
offering the woman's body. In the Bible too there is a connection
between fruit and female sexuality.[6] A naked woman offers a naked man
fruit that opens the eyes so that they *know* they are naked. Knowledge in

in Ancient Israel (Minneapolis: Fortress Press, 1997), pp. 123-93. More recent readings
have been critical of claims made for gender equality in Gen. 2–3 by early feminist
interpreters; see, e.g., Clines, *What Does Eve Do to Help?*, pp. 25-48; Fewell and Gunn,
Gender, Power and Promise, pp. 22-38; Milne, 'The Patriarchal Stamp of Scripture'; and
Lanser, '(Feminist) Criticism in the Garden'.
  4.   Trible, *God and the Rhetoric of Sexuality*, p. 114.
  5.   For this translation of *shema' beqol*, see p. 25 n. 29 above.
  6.   See above, p. 33.

such a context could be seen as an allusion to sexual intercourse.[7] In the biblical text Eve is primarily connected to the body whereas Adam is brought from the ground. Eve is brought forth from Adam's body:

> This at last is bone of my bones
> and flesh of my flesh;
> she shall be called woman
> because from man she was taken (Gen. 2.23).

Eve's punishment in the text is connected to her sexuality. She has to endure painful childbirth and she will desire her dominating husband sexually. In the biblical text, as in advertising, female sexuality is threatening. The biblical text tries to control it by blaming the woman and then having her ruled by her husband. Advertising also tries to control female sexuality, as well as to harness it and exploit it. The same danger and threat portrayed in the biblical text are present in advertising images of Eve: women are blamed for male desire, and for leading men astray. In the text, although the consequences of Adam and Eve's transgression are not all negative, woman must still be controlled. Although advertising celebrates Eve's transgression and her sexuality, it also, insidiously, controls women by defining for them a particular role. It tells women that their most important attribute is their sexuality. In order to have status and acquire wealth and power, a woman must be both attractive to men and more attractive than other women. Advertising purports to be empowering women with a female-defined sexuality but in reality male interests are so deeply embedded in culture that it would difficult for women to create subjective representations of their sexuality without seeing themselves through male eyes. Margaret Miles comments:

> The female body which has played such a central historical role in the circulation of meaning in the Christian West is perhaps too assimilated to the male gaze to permit inscription with new meaning, with a female-defined sexuality and subjectivity. Female nakedness is, after all, at least as vigorously appropriated to the male gaze in the twentieth century media culture as it ever was.

Instead of offering women new or alternative ways of viewing themselves, advertising rehashes old images and old stereotypes. It changes only the blurb. While female sexuality, as defined by Eve in postfeminist advertising images, remains sexuality defined by androcentric concerns, the

---

7. The verb *yada'* is a term for sexual intercourse; see Brown, Driver and Briggs, *A Hebrew and English Lexicon of the Old Testament*, p. 394a; and the D.J.A. Clines (ed.), *Dictionary of Classical Hebrew* (8 vols.; Sheffield: Sheffield Phoenix Press, 1993–2011), IV, p. 100b.

advertisers have a different agenda from that of the biblical text, with its concern to preserve patriarchal hierarchy. Where the Bible is concerned with keeping women in their place, advertising is concerned with making money. The representations of Adam in advertising merely underscore the importance of sexuality in the images of Eve. They are the exceptions that prove the rule, and the fact that a male naked body can mean something so different from a female naked body is testament to the deeply embedded gender stereotypes prevalent in popular culture and, I would argue, rooted in the biblical text.

The Serpent Beguiled Me and I Ate

In postfeminist advertising, the male domination of old is overthrown in favour of women taking control of the representation of their sexuality and using it for their own financial and social gain. The more attractive a woman is, the more successful and powerful she is; however, this state of success and empowerment can only be achieved by women through consumption of commodity goods. Women can only become, and remain, sexually attractive by buying perfume, wearing the right clothing, the right make-up, the right underwear. This active self-commodification and objectification, the advertisements suggest, will increase women's social status and economic power, a point made by sociologist Robert Goldman in his book, *Reading Ads Socially*:

> Her appearance is her value, and her avenue to accumulating capital. Ironically, men once dominated women on the basis of proprietary claims made on the body of woman; today, male domination gets reproduced on the basis of women acquiring proprietary control over their own bodies—or, over the appearances given off by their bodies.[8]

It is not enough to be sexually attractive, however. To achieve financial and social success a woman must be more sexually attractive than other women, she must participate in a competition to attract the gaze and hold it. This competition inevitably means that women become more isolated from each other, losing their collective political power, because every other woman is a threat to the power achieved through self-commodification. Power achieved through self-commodification of sexuality must continually be pursued, it is a never-ending task. Therefore, images of Eve as postfeminist icon are as much about female envy as they are about female sexual power. Female power, according to these adverts, can only come about through desirable sexuality and desirable

8. Goldman, *Reading Ads Socially*, p. 123.

sexuality can only come about through consumerism. In Eve images, as in all postfeminist advertising images targeted to the female market sector, power and success can only be achieved through consumerism. In short, in postfeminist popular culture, consumerism *is* power. The downside of this female empowerment through (hetero)sexuality is that it is an expensive and time-consuming task. Women must fight to achieve status through sexuality, continually measuring themselves against other women, continually updating the latest fashion, the latest make-up, the latest skin-care or exercise regime, continually striving to become more sexually attractive, continually consuming to become a more profitable commodity.

Since postfeminist advertising is concerned primarily with social status, power and female sexual and financial independence, many Eve advertisements feature a female celebrity playing the role of Eve. These celebrities exemplify the very concept that postfeminist advertising is trying to sell: female sexuality is the route to increased wealth, power and status. For instance, one of the highest paid models in the world, Naomi Campbell, takes the role of Eve in the 2005 Ford StreetKa advert (Fig. 3.0):

Figure 3.0. *Print Advertisement for the Ford StreetKa Roadster, 2005*

This advertisement shows Campbell in a Garden of Eden setting, standing in front of a red open-top Ford StreetKa Roadster. The by-line to the image is 'The Sinful New Roadster'. Campbell wears only a fig-leaf, and long hair extensions obscure her breasts from view. She is holding a snake around her neck, and she looks directly into the camera, fixing the viewer's gaze with her own.

Campbell, one of the original supermodels, was chosen for the StreetKa advertising campaign after Ford's marketing research showed that the target consumers (again the 18–34 females) for their new soft-top roadster thought the most attractive temptress of our time was Naomi Campbell. Well-known in the media for being both beautiful and confrontational,[9] Campbell has a reputation for being a diva—a highly paid, successful female celebrity who is prone to being very difficult and demanding. The connection of the Ford StreetKa Roadster with the concept of temptation, which is connoted by the Garden of Eden set, and the choice of Campbell to model as Eve, the most desirable female celebrity to most young women consumers, suggests to those consumers that the car is as desirable as Campbell. Campbell, the advert suggests, would not only be the kind of woman to drive this car, beautiful, successful, wealthy, sexually desirable, feisty, but she finds the car incredibly desirable. The car is positioned as the apple in the image; both Campbell and the StreetKa Roadster are objects of temptation but the car is even more tempting than the ultimate contemporary temptress herself. The consumer is positioned as Adam and Campbell is simultaneously tempting us with herself (both her legendary body and her persona) and with the StreetKa 'apple'. 'If you drive this, you will appear as desirable and successful as Campbell', the advert suggests. The ordinary young women who are the target consumers of this car are not supermodels, they are unlikely to be wealthy,[10] but they would want to be seen as sexually desirable, feisty and successful. The advertisement tells them that buying this car will allow them to achieve their aspirations.

Two advertisements illustrate a further technique to link the woman in Eve advertisements with the poison of the apple or the appeal of the serpent. By matching the shade of the serpent (Fig. 3.1) or the apple

9.   Campbell had been ordered to attend anger-management classes by a judge after an employee had taken her to court for allegedly verbally abusing and hitting her. This was before Campbell was ordered to do community service for attacking another employee in a different court case.

10.   The car was designed for 18–24 year olds and is in the lowest price bracket for a new car, and even though this would still be too much for the target group, it could certainly be bought one by their parents as their first car.

(Fig. 3.2), with the symbolic red lips of Eve, the connection between female sexual anatomy and the forbidden fruit or the 'evil' serpent is made clear. In the advertisement for the Boucheron fragrance *Trouble* the effect is emphasized further by the cropping of the woman so that her lips are the main feature of the image. This emphasizes the lips of the woman and results in the image not representing an individual woman but representing the dangerous sexual qualities of women in general.

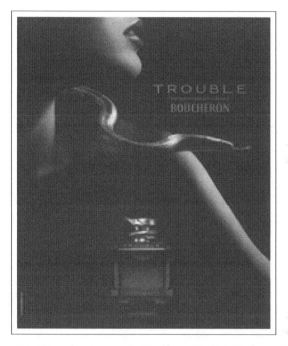

Figure 3.1. *Print advertisement for Boucheron* Trouble *Perfume, 2002*

In Figure 3.1 the serpent and the perfume bottle are matched perfectly with the woman's parted lips. The shared colour of the woman's mouth, the serpent and the perfume bottle creates a link between the snake in the Garden of Eden story and woman's sexuality, equating that sexuality with 'trouble'. In the image, Eve is truly a troublesome helpmate. However, the cropping of the woman's face, while enhancing the lips, dehumanizes the woman and removes her ability to confer the idea that she has power to the viewer via her look. In postfeminist Eve images, the concept of power—achieved through self-objectification and being sexually desirable to the consumer—is conveyed through Eve's return of the male gaze. In the Boucheron advertisement, Eve is prevented from conveying power because her eyes are cropped. She is rendered powerless, while still representing sexual temptation, the male desire for the female and the destruction of the male (the 'trouble' referred to in the advertisement's strap-line) through that desire. The power that the advertisement suggests—the power to attract through female sexuality—is domesticated by the denial of Eve's return gaze.

Figure 3.2. *Print advertisement for TSUM Department Store, Russia, 2010*

Similarly, in the advertising campaign for Russian luxury department store TSUM (Fig. 3.2), which features supermodel Cindy Crawford in various states of undress lounging on a double-bed, the theme is temptation. Crawford, as Eve, holds an apple matched with her lipstick, the two points of colour in an otherwise monochromatic scheme. She tempts the viewer sexually with her forbidden fruit, but she also tempts the female consumer into aspiring to be like her by shopping at TSUM and buying the clothes she models.

In an advertisement for Lolita Lempicka's *The First Fragrance*, the female return gaze is once again prohibited (Fig. 3.3). The image depicts a fantasy woodland scene, in which a woman in a torn evening dress lies on the trunk of tree, with one hand covering her exposed right breast and the other holding her head in a posture that seems to be a swoon or an expression of what could be either post-coital pleasure or post-traumatic distress.

Figure 3.3. *Print Advertisement for* The First Fragrance *by Lolita Lempicka, 2001*

The woman's bare legs, abdomen and breast suggest that she has been involved in a sexual encounter. The image is ambiguous, however, about whether that encounter was violent or of mutual consent. The positioning of the perfume bottle near her feet connects the ambiguous sexual scene with the apple containing the first fragrance. As usual in post-feminist Eve advertisements, the apple connotes the forbidden fruit in

Genesis 3 and links the image of the ravished woman with temptation and desire. Is this an image of Eve after she has eaten of the fruit of the knowledge of good and evil? If so, where is Adam? Whatever the story of the advertisement, the reason for the exhausted, prone, half-naked and dishevelled state of Eve is the effect of the first fragrance. The spectator-buyer sees that using the first fragrance can make a woman so sexually desirable that she will attract aggressive sexual attention, whether that attention is invited or otherwise. On its appearance in women's glossy magazines, the ambiguity of the advertisement and the suggestion of sexual assault—and indeed the insinuation of the image that sexual assault might be a desired outcome by women who wish to be considered highly sexually attractive—led feminist groups to protest against the image and petition for its removal from circulation. In fact, the publicity surrounding the image significantly increased the profile of the perfume and Lolita Lempicka won a prestigious Fifi advertising award for best advertising campaign at the 2001 fragrance awards.

Images of suggested sexual violence are commonplace in postfeminist advertising,[11] having become

> ...romantic and chic instead of being seen as grievously contemptible. Such ads are used by some of the most reputable manufacturers in mainstream magazines aimed at refined, stylish audiences... Ads convey the message that...women secretly want to be raped, and that women invite rape by their behaviour and attire.[12]

11.   See also the double-page advertising image for *Agent Provocateur* underwear, depicting a murder scene in which a woman's body, wearing a transparent net bra, suspenders and stilettos, is sprawled on stairs. Her body is cordoned off with crime scene tape. The suggestion is that wearing *Agent Provocateur* underwear can have such a dramatic impact that it could cause one of its customers to be murdered. See *Agent Provocateur*'s promotional coffee-table book, Joseph Corré and Serena Rees, *Agent Provocateur: A Celebration of Femininity* (London: Carlton, 1999), pp. 168-69.

12.   Cortese, *Provocateur*, p. 73. The idea that a woman and even a child bears responsibility for provoking a sexual attack is still in evidence in court cases in the UK. Most recently (25 June 2007) a 24-year-old window cleaner, Keith Fenn, was given a minimal custodial sentence of three and half years for two counts of raping a ten-year-old girl in a park. Due to the amount of time Fenn had already spent in prison awaiting his sentence, the sentence would mean that he only had to spend another four months in imprisonment for the crimes. In his summing up of the trial, Judge Julian Hall QC said that the girl looked sixteen and was 'sexually precocious' and that the child dressed 'provocatively'. In a previous child abuse case in February 2007, however, Hall suggested that compensation paid to a child-abuse victim could be used to buy the child a bicycle to 'cheer them up'. See Mark Tran, 'Call for Appeal over "Pathetically Lenient" Rape Sentence', *The Guardian* (25 June 2007).

Such advertisements display the flip-side of self-objectification in a society that still blames victims of sexual assault for attracting the 'wrong kind' of attention.[13] Rather than resisting, problematizing or challenging such gender-biased attitudes, advertisements such as the one for Lolita Lempicka *The First Fragrance* help perpetuate the notion that a woman invites and welcomes all sexual attention from men, even rape, reflecting widespread sexist social attitudes to female victims of sexual assault and abuse.

The updated version of the Lolita Lempicka *The First Fragrance* advertisement displays a similar, if less obviously controversial, ideology to the previous image (Fig. 3.4). Once again, Eve is pictured in a fantasy woodland scene but this time she sits on the trunk of the tree, looking sideways into the distance. As before, the advertisers have chosen to have the model look away from the viewer. She looks into the distance, or at a person off-scene, and her expression seems unhappy. Light falls on her exposed bare legs and her face. The advertisement is once again ambiguous—not only does the woman wear a torn dress, similar to the one 'Eve' wears in the previous advertisement, but she appears to have a bruise on her left cheek-bone. This could be heavily applied make-up, but, given the torn dress, the sad expression of the young woman and the supposed 'overwhelming' effect of using the fragrance, one has reason to wonder. The light upon her face has bleached her eye make-up to the point where only half her eye-brow is visible; any make-up to enhance a cheek-bone should be bleached or at least have a much more subtle effect also. Whether the viewer decides that the mark is make-up or bruising is actually of less importance than the fact that the advertisement creates

---

13.   See the following scholarly works for further examples of this attitude to victims of sexual violence: D. Abrams *et al.*, 'Evaluating Stranger and Acquaintance Rape: The Role of Benevolent Sexism in Perpetrator Blame and Recommended Sentence Length', *Law & Human Behavior* 3.28 (2004), pp. 295-303; D. Abrams *et al.*, 'Perceptions of Stranger and Acquaintance Rape: The Role of Benevolent and Hostile Sexism in Victim Blame and Rape Proclivity', *Journal of Personality & Social Psychology* 1.84 (2003), pp. 111-25; Helen Benedict, *Virgin or Vamp: How the Press Covers Sex Crimes* (Oxford: Oxford University Press, 1992); G. Bohner and N. Schwarz, 'The Threat of Rape: Its Psychological Impact on Non-victimized Women', in D.M. Buss and N. Malamuth (eds.), *Sex, Power, Conflict: Evolutionary and Feminist Perspectives* (Oxford: Oxford University Press, 1996), pp. 162-75; K.K.P. Johnson, 'Attributions about Date Rape: Impact of Clothing, Sex, Money Spent, Date Type, and Perceived Similarity', *Family and Consumer Sciences Research Journal* 23 (1995), pp. 292-311; G. Tendayi Viki and Dominic Abrams, 'But She Was Unfaithful: Benevolent Sexism and Reactions to Rape Victims Who Violate Traditional Gender Role Expectations—Brief Report', *Sex Roles: A Journal of Research* 47 (2002), pp. 289-93.

enough ambiguity to suggest that the woman could have been the victim of an aggressive encounter.

The image could depict the scene after the first Lolita Lempicka advertisement, when the woman was able to recover from her experience, but the Company has used a different model and her hair is styled differently. Whereas in the first advertisement the woman's hair-style was long loose curls, thrown over her upper face, after a dramatic sexual encounter, this woman's hair-style is far more groomed. She has flowers fixed into the side of her hair and the style seems to be still in place regardless of whatever happened to shred her dress or result in possible facial bruising. While the advertisements may be ambiguous as to what has actually taken place immediately before the scenes they portray, they leave the spectator-buyer in no doubt about the power of the fragrance to make women overwhelmingly sexually desirable.

Figure 3.4. *Print advertisement for* The First Fragrance *by Lolita Lempicka, 2003*

The Lolita Lempicka advertisements are unusual in terms of the pattern of representation in postfeminist Eve advertisements, however, because the models do not return the consumer's male gaze. Usually in postfeminist advertising, the models' acknowledgment and direct return of the viewers' gaze is a technique to convey not only the power of the woman in the image but also to signify resistance and challenge to traditional patriarchal social values, as Robert Goldman concluded in his study of 1980s and early 1990s advertising:

[Postfeminist advertising] reinforces a prominent ideological account of woman defined by the male gaze. The ability to survey is based on power, but here the female look confers power. Women's power over man is thus ironically depicted as a function of her willing acceptance of her vulnerability and powerlessness *vis-à-vis men*. Here, the woman as paragon of beauty commands the male's attention by making herself *an object* of desire.[14]

Such a fine line differentiates passive 'sexist' female objectification from postfeminist self-objectification that promotes female sexuality as a means to achieve power and success that postfeminist advertising images must attribute sexual agency to Eve in order to show that she is active and powerful in her objectification rather than passive and powerless.

For instance, like Lolita Lempicka, the perfume company Cacharel chose to use Eve imagery to represent their notion of desirable contemporary femininity. Also like Lolita Lempicka, the company updated its print advertisement to one that offered the same garden of Eden theme but enabled a slightly different reading.

Figure 3.5. *Print advertisement for* Eden *perfume, Cacharel, 1995*

14. Goldman, *Reading Ads Socially*, p. 117 (emphasis original).

Figure 3.5 is the first print advertisement for Cacharel's perfume, *Eden: The Forbidden Fragrance*. In the image Eve returns the viewer's gaze; how-ever, her expression seems to be questioning the look of the spectator-buyer rather than obviously inviting it. At the same time, however, she also displays the forbidden perfume by holding it next to her exposed left breast, linking the idea of forbidden pleasure with both the bottle of fragrance and the woman's naked body.

Figure 3.6. *Print advertisement for* Eden *perfume, Cacharel, 2000*

In the updated print advertisement for the same fragrance (Fig. 3.6), Cacharel's advertisers have chosen to make the overall impression of the image a little darker and more dangerous. The very name of the perfume 'El Perfume Prohibido' (The Forbidden Fragrance) suggests that the per-fume will cause illicit or illegal consequences for the wearer. The second advert makes more of this notion than the first.

Both representations have cast Eve in a greenish-blue light. The second advertisement puts this colour against hot shades of orange and yellow and a brighter green, whereas the first image placed Eve against a backdrop of pastel colours and gave Eve an innocent look, with a coiffed and quite androgynous hairstyle (making her more innocent looking, despite her bare breast and the 'El Perfume Prohibido' tag-line). The updated image presents a new version of Eve, a tousled-haired, pouty-lipped woman who does not display her breast to the viewer, but instead offers the spectator-buyer a tantalising suggestion of breast, just available for view under her slightly lifted arm. Although she may turn her back on the gaze, she does not turn her face—she returns the viewer's gaze with a knowing pout. She does not question the gaze, as her predecessor did; in fact, the image presents this version of Eve as if the viewer has surprised her. Now she knows we are looking, and she is complicit in the game of looking because the increased sexual attraction created by her looking is the desired effect of the forbidden perfume.

The promise of increased sexual attraction and the implicit promise of increased power with which it is associated is characteristic of postfeminist advertising. The power the advertisements promise to the spectator-buyer, however, is illusory. Postfeminist advertisements focus on the individual rather than the collective ability of women to create improvements in their lives. In these advertisements, the individual woman's body becomes the site of liberation and route for achieving power. The advertising constructs a femininity that is organized around sexual confidence and autonomy and promotes this femininity as an embrace of the assertive, liberated woman, the powerful *femme fatale* who debilitates men with her overwhelming sexuality. This femininity, however, allows the women who subscribe to postfeminist advertising ideology only tokens of power that are dependent on whether or not the woman competes for male attention, maintains her gender performance as sexually desirable temptress and participates in the constant consumerism that this brand of postfeminism necessitates. L.S. Kim warns against the dangers of self-objectification in her discussion of postfeminism in television:

> Moving from passive object of the male gaze to self-objectification does not necessarily achieve subjectivity, and it can be a false freedom. Self-objectification could be defined as the conscious effort to gain attention through one's feminine traits—again, sexual attention, not professional attention.[15]

When a woman's sexuality becomes her ultimate tool for the achievement of power and social status, women are dissuaded from forming collective groups—the groups that really can achieve power shifts and

15. L.S. Kim, '"Sex and the Single Girl" in Postfeminism: The F Word on Television', *Television and New Media* 2.4 (November 2001), p. 324.

increase women's social status—to challenge the socio-political condi-
tions that make male/female child-care responsibilities still heavily
imbalanced for women, that allow a pay-structure in which women
consistently earn a lower salary than men for the same job[16] and that
maintain that women's best chance of achieving power and increasing
social status is through exploiting the market value of their own sexuality. In effect, postfeminist advertising ideology depoliticizes women's
struggles for power in daily life and purports that women's power issues
can be solved through consumerism. Issues of gender equality are no
longer about pay, unequal child-care, discrimination, sexual harassment,
domestic abuse and so on, but become questions about the most effective
perfume, underwear, chocolate or clothing to offer increased sexual
desirability. The suggestion of postfeminist advertising is that the better
looking a woman is, and the more she maintains her gender performance,
the less she will struggle with the issues that 'normal' women have to
contend with in life.

Figure 3.7. *Print advertisement for Thorntons Eden Chocolates
in* Glamour *magazine, February 2003*

16.   See Bunting, 'Baby, This Just Isn't Working for Me'.

As this book has so far argued, consumerism is the foundation of post-feminist advertising ideology, which links female power and resistance to traditional patriarchal values by means of self-objectification. Advertisers use Eve imagery to exploit *femme fatale* imagery and transform it into an image of contemporary female sexual empowerment through consumerism. A double-page advertisement for Thorntons Eden chocolates, which appeared in *Glamour* magazine in February 2003 makes the postfeminist advertising agenda I have been discussing so far in this book particularly explicit by virtue of the connections it makes between female sexual temptation and consumer empowerment. In the promotional article (Fig. 3.10) from *Glamour* Magazine in 2003, the link between Eve, young women and luxury products is made clear. The advertisement was included in the magazine as a triple page advertisement (the third page was a full page picture of the Thorntons Eden chocolates that the article was promoting). The first page shows the image of a young woman of the same age range as the target reader of the magazine (age 17–25) (Fig. 3.7). She is pictured from the waist up and she is naked, with her right arm covering her breasts. Although she covers her breasts with her arm and hand, the photo still allows much of her cleavage to be available for view by the spectator-buyer. The inside of the chocolate is red, which matches the shade of her lips, linking the forbidden fruit with the young woman herself. She is positioned as a temptation to the consumer in the same way as the chocolate; her function is to attract and to be consumed. The image suggests that the viewer has just caught Eve as she is about to bite into the forbidden fruit (the particular chocolate she is holding is actually called 'Forbidden Fruit' in the menu of Eden chocolates). Eve returns the spectator-buyer's gaze, although her expression is not welcoming—her look is simultaneously seductive (she is pouting rather than scowling or being pictured with her mouth open ready to eat the chocolate) and hostile—because, as the advertising copy suggests, the viewer has just interrupted her 'being bad' (Fig. 3.8):

> We all have the right to be sinful sometimes, and we've uncovered the most deliciously decadent gift to entice and seduce in serious style. Get your wicked way, and you'll be glad to be bad. Here's our guide to uncovering your 'inner-Eve', where no sense is left untouched…[17]

The idea is that pleasure, style, consumer temptation and luxury products are all part of what a young woman needs to do to make herself feel good. The constant consumption of expensive luxury goods is naturalized in

17. Print Advertisement for Eden Chocolates by Thorntons, *Glamour* Magazine (February 2003).

these adverts. The young women reading this magazine may very well not have the means to afford luxury goods but that is not seen as an obstacle when the encoded message is that buying expensive things may be naughty but 'we all have the right to be sinful sometimes'.[18]

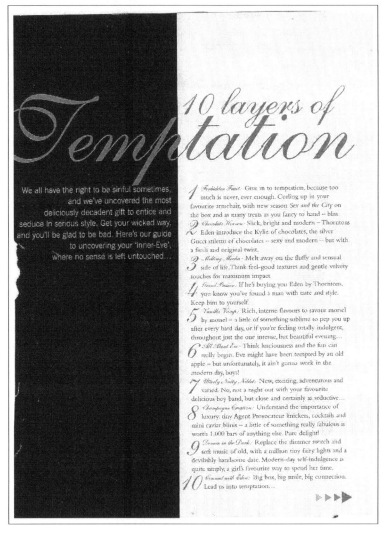

Figure 3.8. *Print advertisement for Eden Chocolates by Thorntons,* Glamour *magazine, February 2003*

18. '10 Layers of Temptation', Thorntons Advertisement, *Glamour* Magazine (February 2003).

The advertisement shows an image of Eve, in which chocolate has been substituted for the forbidden fruit, on one page, and describes the '10 Layers of Temptation' on the other.

The '10 Layers of Temptation' refers to the ten chocolates in a box of Thorntons confectionary and alludes to another well-established biblical trope, the Ten Commandments. Each chocolate has a name, the advertisement's copy lists each of the chocolates by its Eden-inspired name, and offers young women ways to 'uncover their inner-Eve' through self-indulgence.

The first 'layer', Forbidden Fruit, suggests that *Glamour*'s readers 'give in to temptation, because too much is never, ever enough. Curling up in your favourite armchair, with new season *Sex and the City* on the box and as many treats as you fancy to hand—bliss.' The advertising copy links Thorntons chocolates with postfeminist ideology of empowerment through sexuality and consumerism. By mentioning *Sex and the City* the advertisers suggest to the *Glamour* reader that Thorntons Eden chocolates are in the same bracket as the popular postfeminist television show. *Sex and the City*, HBO's phenomenally successful TV series, was at its peak of popularity in 2003. It centred around four female friends and their relationship, sex and wardrobe issues. By associating the two brands, Thorntons Eden chocolates and *Sex and the City*, with each other in the copy, the advertisers of Thorntons Eden hope to associate their product with the same 'cool' qualities as *Sex and the City*: sex and consumerism.[19] Another 'layer of temptation' cements this connection between luxury consumer brands and Thorntons Eden Chocolates by saying that the advertised confectionary is 'the silver Gucci stiletto of chocolates—sexy and modern—but with a fresh and original twist'. The copy then goes on to create connections between the Thorntons chocolates and consumer indulgence with the vague direction for readers to 'Think lusciousness and the fun can really begin. Eve might have been tempted by an old apple—but unfortunately it ain't gonna work in the modern day, boys!' So, although the advertisement is targeting young female postfeminist

19. For more comprehensive discussions of *Sex and the City* as a postfeminist text, see Kim, '"Sex and the Single Girl"'; Yvonne Tasker and Diane Negra, 'In Focus: Postfeminism and Contemporary Media Studies', *Cinema Journal* 44 (2005), pp. 107-10; Diane Negra, '"Quality Postfeminism?" Sex and the Single Girl on HBO', *Genders Online Journal* 39 (2004) (http://www.genders.org [accessed 21 February 2005]); Rachel Moseley and Jacinda Read, '"Having it *Ally*": Popular Television (Post-)Feminism', *Feminist Media Studies* (2002), pp. 231-49, and Amanda D. Lotz, 'Postfeminist Television Criticism: Rehabilitating Critical Terms and Identifying Postfeminist Attributes', *Feminist Media Studies* 1.1 (2001), pp. 105-21.

consumers in a young women's magazine, it assumes that the young women are receiving gifts from men. In order to tempt these young women into transgression, the advert suggests, the men are going to have to buy them something that presumably runs along the same lines as the Gucci shoes that have been mentioned in the copy. Is this alluding to the power that postfeminism promises women in return for self-objectification? The power to achieve male financial support through being sexually desirable? The postfeminist idea of female empowerment through sexuality does not seem altogether too different from the husband-hunting that nineteenth century women had to go through in order to be financially secure.[20] For those women, trying to find the most eligible male to be a husband created competition among women and ensured that collective groups of women were unlikely to be formed because of the threat each woman posed to others. Similarly, postfeminism creates competition between women in terms of who can be the most successful temptress. Postfeminism can only benefit individual women, not women as a collective, since postfeminist advertising ideology is fundamentally exclusive: only the attractive, young, able-bodied and those who can give the appearance of being wealthy can participate in the competition for power.

At the end of the '10 Layers of Temptation', the Thorntons advertisement goes on to expose the deceit of postfeminist advertising ideology: 'Champagne Creation: Understand the importance of luxury: tiny *Agent Provocateur* knickers, cocktails and mini caviar blinis—a little of something really fabulous is worth 1,000 bars of anything else. Pure delight!' The advertisement describes luxuries that only a small percentage of young women aged between 18–25 could possibly afford, and yet these items are listed as if they are part of everyday self-indulgence for the *Glamour* reader—or if they are not then they should be. The underwear company mentioned by the Thorntons advertisement is currently a highly fashionable, highly expensive underwear manufacturer, who leads the way in postfeminist advertising. In their promotional coffee-table book, *Agent Provocateur: A Celebration of Femininity*,[21] the company's creators, Joseph Corré and Serena Rees, express the basic tenets of postfeminist consumer ideology eloquently:

20.   See Showalter, *Sexual Anarchy*, p. 100.

21.   Significantly for this book, Agent Provocateur means 'spies who provoke others to act illegally', which reflects the same theme as Eve advertising—that through the manipulation and display of her sexuality a woman can provoke others to act illegally or transgressively. This is a basic theme of postfeminism and the reason why Eve has become a postfeminist icon.

> At a time when political correctness has created an anti-individual environment to avoid offending anyone and when companies only act on ideas after the approval of marketing men, the aptly named *Agent Provocateur* was created to redress the balance. In a democracy where your only real choice is where you spend your money ('I shop therefore I am'), we found it necessary to open an outlet that we could use as a platform for our ideas and where we could provokingly display the sexuality of the female form without embarrassment or shame.[22]

The idea that collective politics has been superseded by individual consumer choice is inherent in all postfeminist advertising, as is the fundamental fantasy that women have achieved professional and personal equality in contemporary society and so should inevitably make a return to 'femininity', which always involves the constant consumption of clothes, cosmetics, shoes and perfume. *Agent Provocateur*'s statements expose the serious discrepancies in postfeminist advertising ideology: the idea that women have achieved equality but still need to be sold ways to achieve power is ironic, as is the idea that women can afford expensive luxury items in order to achieve this power when they are yet to receive the same salary as men for the same job. Women, contrary to what the creators of *Agent Provocateur* want us to believe, are far from equally represented in the highest professional offices in academia—medicine, law and politics—a fact that Corré and Rees totally dismiss in their promotional literature:

> That women would rise to the heights of corporate, academic, and artistic success was inevitable. Women were no longer objects of seduction but powerful and provocative seducers, as well as highly competent professionals. With the power of equality, and the right and ability to choose, there was a yearning to return to an expression of femininity that has been put aside in order to succeed. It was time for a return to femininity by exploiting female charm, and what better way to draw attention to female power than by emphasising the female form? We believe that the ultimate expression is for each individual woman to emphasize her femininity and to revel in her erotic life. After all, the instinct to display and attract is inescapable. The desire to be sexy and the innate sexiness of the body remain, no matter how it is politicized. If you've got it, flaunt it. If you don't have it, GET SOME![23]

The idea expressed in this quotation from Corré and Rees—that women can buy sexiness, charm and thereby achieve female power (If you don't have it. GET SOME!)—is the concept that fuels postfeminist Eve advertising.

22.   Corré and Rees, *Agent Provocateur*, p. 7.
23.   Corré and Rees, *Agent Provocateur*, pp. 43-44.

As we saw in Chapter 2, the irony for women subscribing to the notion of female empowerment through self-commodification and sexualization is that, in participating in 'empowerment through consumerism' to become a more profitable commodity, in reality young women can suffer a tremendous loss. The difficulty for women who identify themselves with postfeminist values and view their bodies and sexuality as their most valuable commodities is that, because self-commodification leads to extreme competition among females, very few at any one time are successful in achieving power and wealth through their bodies. The few who are successful will change rapidly because the nature of consumerism is that what is considered desirable one year may well be passé the next, and the women who are fighting for their market share will have to work hard to ensure they maintain male desire and female envy. For instance, the most successful sexual-saleswomen at the moment are Beyonce Knowles, Jennifer Lopez and Scarlett Johansson—all of whom have developed themselves into the ultimate commodity: an identity brand.[24] These women are no longer only actresses and singers, their very identity is a commodity. This identity brand is based solely on the desirability of the women; the consumer has to want what these celebrities have. Johansson has a dizzying list of celebrity endorsements increasing her wealth each year: Calvin Klein fragrances, Dolce and Gabbana and Moet Chandon to name but a few of the most lucrative. She is also a 'spokesmodel' for the cosmetics giant L'Oreal, as is Knowles.

The companies hiring these female celebrities choose them because of their ability to represent the qualities they want associated with the product. For instance, L'Oreal wants to appeal to young, popular-culture literate, financially independent women. Thus they offer contracts to young female celebrities who are in the media eye, are considered highly desirable and attractive by consumers and who have achieved their status through their looks—perfect for a cosmetics company. In her press statement after accepting the L'Oreal contract, Johansson said, 'It is wonderful to be working with L'Oreal, a company that has celebrated

---

24. Both Beyonce Knowles and Jennifer Lopez are known to work out for two hours per day and have extremely restrictive diets to maintain their desirable and marketable figures. Knowles, in particular, has attracted criticism for admitting that she eats only slices of tomato and cucumber for lunch to keep body-fat to a minimum and fasted on a liquid-only diet to lose two stones for her part as the lead singer, Dinah, in the recent, hugely hyped and Academy Award winning *Dreamgirls* movie.

independent women for years',[25] making clear the link between cosmetics, consumerism and female independence.[26]

Knowles's and Lopez's skills of self-commodification are formidable, with both of them flooding the market with popular film and album releases, appearing in numerous advertising campaigns and launching their own fashion, make-up and perfume lines. These women know how to sell themselves. They are the proof of the power of sexual objectification and they are the role models for current and future consumers. Significantly, Knowles, Lopez and Britney Spears, all known for their overt sexuality and all highly successful identity brands, appeared together in a 2004 TV commercial for Pepsi that was shown during the Super Bowl. The commercial showed the three women as gladiators who were about to fight in a contest, again linking commodified female sexuality with power and strength. The commercial was one of the most successful of all time.

Advertisers are not creating a link between commodified female sexuality and independence, wealth, power and social status that is not apparent to the target young female consumer herself: in the 2006 Forbes Celebrity 100 Power list, which lists the most influential celebrities each year, there were proportionately few women compared to the number of men. Tom Cruise was at number one and the top two women were Oprah Winfrey and J.K. Rowling, at numbers three and nineteen respectively. Most of the women on the list had made their name through their looks. On the Forbes website each celebrity on the most influential list has their two most marketable assets listed next to their picture.[27] Four of the celebrities on the list were models, Gisele Bundchen, Kate Moss, Tyra Banks and Heidi Klum, and they each had 'beautiful, sexy' or 'attractive, stylish' next to their photos. These women have become

25.   Http://www.imdb.com/news/wenn/2006-01-05#celeb6.

26.   In Reebok's statement to the press, released after hiring Johanssen to endorse one of their footwear ranges, Reebok describes the Hollywood star as a 'world renowned style icon' and 'an inspiration for today's young women', making clear the link between celebrities who commodify their sexuality to achieve a market value and the appeal of these celebrities to young women. Reebok wanted to exploit that link to achieve greater customer sales, knowing that young women would be more likely to purchase a product that was endorsed by Johanssen in an attempt to emulate her appeal. See BusinessWire, 'Reebok Partners with Screen Star Scarlett Johansson to Create Red-Hot Fashion Collection, Scarlett Hearts Rbk' (22 July 2006).

27.   Http://www.forbes.com/2006/06/12/06celebrities_money-power-celebrities-list_land.html (accessed 21 January 2006).

powerful through being willing to participate in self-objectification and they were being rewarded handsomely for it. Indeed, Gisele Bundchen, currently the highest paid model in the world and number seventy-one on Forbes's list, is worth $30 million for being 'beautiful, sexy'. Forbes goes on to say that Bundchen has 'twenty fashion contracts and her "assets" earned her more last year than many of the highest paid actors on the Celebrity 100'.[28]

To succeed in popular culture women must be attractive and willing to exploit their attractiveness for its maximum market potential. This allows women to be powerful and wealthy, but still nowhere near as powerful as men, even if the women are out-earning them. Ironically, the two most powerful women on the list, and the only women in the top twenty, Oprah Winfrey and J.K. Rowling, earn far more than any other women on the list (Winfrey is described as earning $275 million and Rowling $75 million) and are described as having far more power and influence than any other woman on the list; however, they are also the only women who do not have any of the tags 'beautiful', 'sexy', 'attractive', 'stylish' or 'cute' next to their names as reasons for their success. Winfrey's most marketable qualities are described as 'intelligent, confident' and Rowling is 'talented, intelligent'. Their place on the list and the personal qualities that have led them to become so wealthy and influential simultaneously undermine and underline postfeminist advertising's notion that the locus of women's power is their sexuality: the most powerful and wealthy women in popular culture have not achieved that status through self-objectification but all the other women on the list have.

There is, however, a negative side to this self-marketing. The demands of successful self-commodification and the constant scrutiny of being the object of the gaze can take their toll on celebrities whose careers, wealth and status are founded on the marketing of their sexuality. Britney Spears, who shot to international stardom with her controversial single, *Baby One More Time*,[29] has made a highly lucrative career from self-objectification. From dancing provocatively in a school uniform replete with mini-skirt and pig-tails in the *Baby One More Time* promotional video, to exploiting the popularity of the Eve image in the MTV 2001 Awards by dancing in a garden of Eden inspired stage set with a python around her neck (the single most reproduced media image of that year),

28. Http://www.forbes.com/2006/06/12/06celebrities_money-power-celebrities-list_land.html (accessed 21 January 2006).
29. Britney Spears, *Baby One More Time* (BMG, 2000).

Spears found status, power, fame and immense wealth through self-objectification.

Marketing herself as a brand, Spears introduced her own clothing range, attached her name to many brands (such as Sketchers shoes and Pepsi) and launched her own perfume.[30] In 2002, at the pinnacle of her career, Spears was named as the world's most powerful celebrity (male and female included) on the Forbes Celebrity 100 list. By 2007, however, Spears had dropped out of the influential Forbes list altogether, thanks to being admitted twice to a celebrity rehabilitation centre for alcohol dependency, two failed marriages, a media furore surrounding her parenting skills and a public breakdown, which saw her shaving her long hair-extensions off while the paparazzi frenziedly photographed the incident. Spears may well still be in the headlines but she is there as an example of a woman whose self-commodification has also caused her self-destruction.

Nevertheless, the drawbacks of female self-promotion through sexuality do not put off the target female 18–35 consumer, who is still attracted to the postfeminist advertising ideology that sells the idea of sex as the ultimate tool to achieve female empowerment. In this climate, images of Eve become ever more popular as a signifier of female independence and power through sexuality. The Eve image often functions as a vehicle, not just for already famous actresses, models and pop stars to connect their persona with the cultural myth of Eve, but for those 'wannabe' celebrity females wishing to become famous through their sexuality.[31]

Eve imagery has been regularly employed in two examples of women who have achieved celebrity status through self-promotion in reality shows or on social media. The first, Allison Melnick, a Los Angeles socialite and friend of Paris Hilton, has created a self-made brand from her famous friends and starring in short-lived reality shows. Melnick frequently uses Eve imagery to market her bar in LA, aptly titled 'Apple', and usually features herself in the bar's promotional material, all of which tends to have an Eve theme, with Melnick presenting herself as the forbidden fruit to be consumed. In the publicity shots for the opening of Apple, Melnick is represented in the standard Eve pose: red apple in

30. Britney Spears's fragrance, *Curious*, has made approximately $100 million in revenue since its launch date in 2004, illustrating the selling-power Spears wielded at the height of her career.

31. The song Britney Spears performed at the MTV Awards in 2001, *Slave 4 U*, was a departure into a new, more adult sound for Spears. It is significant that for this transition from pop queen of the pre-teens to targeting an older audience, Spears's marketing team chose to exploit the Eve image to grab the headlines and make Britney's transformation from sex-kitten to *Femme Fatale* clear.

hand, returning the viewers' gaze. The red shade of the brand logo and the apple she's holding are toned in with Melnick's vest and lipstick, linking her body and mouth with forbidden fruit. On her arm is a tattoo, another of the bar's logos, which shows the outline of a bitten apple under which is written 'bite me'. Here Melnick plays with her sexy but feisty celebrity persona: 'bite me' is a play on words that in the context of the forbidden fruit theme of the advertisement could be a sexual invitation but is also a US idiomatic expression statement to show contempt or defiance. The 'bite me' logo, coupled with the heavy eye-make up and ambivalent facial expression, suggest that she is in control of her sexuality: she simultaneously objectifies herself and offers her body for consumption but distances the viewer with her dual messages.

Figure 3.9. *Apple Restaurant Lounge, 2010*

A further 'reality' celebrity who has used Eve imagery to symbolize her newly advanced status is social media phenomenon Christine Dolce. Figure 3.10 is taken from Dolce's 2006 'Forbidden Fruit' themed Playboy promotional shoot.[32]

Dolce, known as 'ForBiddeN', transformed herself from being a small-town beautician into a million-dollar fitness, fashion and glamour model-ling businesswoman[33] following the huge popularity of her MySpace profile, on which has amassed over two million 'friends' since the launch of the social media site. Dolce's profile and subsequent branding centres around her self-objectification; she posts numerous provocative photos,

32. *Playboy* Magazine (October 2006).
33. See 'ForBiddeN Fruit: Big Business Tries to Make Friends and Influence People Online', *The Economist* (27 June 2006).

regularly updated, which have propelled her to celebrity status. Hailed 'The Queen of MySpace' by *Vanity Fair* magazine[34] and *The Tyra Banks Show*[35] Dolce uses Eve imagery to convey the strength of her sexual appeal to potential consumers but also to signify her postfeminist credentials as a woman who has turned her body into her business purely from posting semi-naked photos of herself on a social media website. Like Melnick, Dolce uses the forbidden fruit as a tool to simultaneously entice and distance the viewer. Dolce's 'brand name' ForBiddeN is as much a warning as the proffered apple and ample cleavage in the Playboy shoot is an invitation. Dolce's use of gothic imagery is part of the distancing technique she employs to counter her self-objectification. Dolce presents herself as a postfeminist vamp, a modern day version of the Poison Damsels from ancient Asian folklore where young women, raised on snake venom so that they become venomous themselves, prove fatal for the men who are seduced by them.[36] This notion of poisonous woman has become conflated in this image with Eve, where the apple signifies the temptation of the viewer but also the *Femme fatale* status of Dolce.

Figure 3.10. *Christine Dolce* Playboy *promotional image*, 2006

34. *Vanity Fair* Magazine (March 2006).
35. *The Tyra Banks Show* (6 April 2006).
36. Allen, *The Femme Fatale*, p. 50.

For example, in Figure 3.11 Dolce represents herself as a forbidden fruit, appealing to look at though she glowers at the viewer, and the word 'FORBIDDEN', written more like a command than a brand name, is typed in between her and the red bitten apple, which is punctured by various piercings—like Dolce's own body—and wrapped in a spiked collar.

Figure 3.11. *Christine Dolce MySpace promotional image, 2006*

From the late 1990s to very recently Eve has been represented as the ultimate postfeminist icon of female sexual power; occasionally, however, her image develops into a more romantic representation of the feminine ideal. Figure 3.12 shows a recent advertisement for the new Nina Ricci perfume *Nina*. The image shows a young, beautiful woman with flowing curled hair in a pink ball gown. Red apples spill from the open door behind her and from a tree above her hangs a perfume bottle in the shape of a red apple. The woman in the image stares with desire at the apple, the by-line is 'le nouveau parfum magique'. Far from being an appeal to women's desire for power, this image appeals to a desire for fantasy and romance. The Nina Ricci website claims the perfume is 'a magical and enchanting fairy tale...an elixir, a promise of enchantment with the radiant power of seduction'.[37]

The progression of the Eve image from *femme fatale* to fairytale princess is a further reflection of the progression of postfeminism. As society becomes ever more concerned with the breakdown of the family structure and the issue of working mothers and its effect on the stability of the family unit, postfeminist advertising images are beginning to lean more towards traditional images of romance, fairytale and fantasy taking women back to a feminine ideal of gentle beauty. The apple, of course, still signifies female individual choice and transformation—as in Figure

37. Nina Ricci website, http://www.ninaricci.com/#/parfums/line_nina/nina (accessed 2 April 2009).

3.12 where it is labelled as 'magic'—but Eve herself has been transformed from temptress to fairytale princess who still desires, although the advertisers' idea of what she must desire has changed. The change in Eve imagery in advertising is not only down to change in issues of post-feminism but also down to the advertisers' need to change the feminine ideals to which women must aspire in order to maintain women's levels of consumption.

In a blow to the postfeminist fairytale of the working-class girl who gets rich and happy from her assets, in 2008 the *Nina* perfume model featured in the advertisement (Fig. 3.12), Ruslana Korshunova, committed suicide[38] and two years later, 21-year-old pop star Florrie was announced as the new 'face' of *Nina L'Elixir* perfume.

Figure 3.12. *Nina Ricci*, Nina, 2006

38.   Melissa Jane Kronfield, 'Supermodel's Death Plunge', *New York Post* (29 June 2008).

Figure 3.13. *Nina Ricci*, Nina L'Elixir, *2010*

The campaign, which included a TV advertisement, is based on 'innocent temptation'[39] where Alice in Wonderland fairytale imagery is conflated with Eve-temptress imagery. In the TV version of the advertisement, Florrie is lying on a white bed, filmed from above, singing Blondie's Sunday Girl. Dressed in an outfit reminiscent of a child's party dress (the same outfit she wears in Fig. 3.13), she moves around a white bedroom before walking coquettishly through a series of bizarre landscapes filled with oversized apples and presents. The advertisement ends when she holds the red, apple-shaped bottle and stares back at the viewer in the standard Eve pose. The Nina Ricci website promotes the fragrance as 'the new outstanding chapter of Nina's fairy tale…sensual and sophisticated like its new modern princess'.[40] The *Nina* advertising campaigns infantilize women consumers, a common technique in advertising throughout its history,[41] domesticating any perceived threat from the temptress, part of what Goffman calls the 'ritualization of subordination'. Goffman's

39.   Nina Ricci website, http://www.ninaricci.com/#/parfums/line_nina/nina_elixirr (accessed 3 April 2009).

40.   Nina Ricci website, http://www.ninaricci.com/#/parfums/line_nina/nina_elixirr (accessed 3 April 2009).

41.   For a longitudinal study of the representation of women in popular culture, including representations in which women are infantilized, see Erin Hatton and Mary Nell Trautner, 'Images of Powerful Women in the Age of "Choice Feminism"', *Journal of Gender Studies* 22.2 (forthcoming 2013).

ritualization of subordination includes the 'the knee bend', as displayed
by Florrie in the *Nina L'Elixir* image (Fig. 3.13):

> Women frequently, men very infrequently, are posed in a display of the
> 'bashful knee bend'. Whatever else, the knee bend can be read as a foregoing
> of full effort to be prepared and on the ready in the current social situation,
> for the position adds a moment of effort to fight or flee. Once again one finds
> a posture that seems to presuppose the goodwill of anyone in the surround
> who could offer harm. Observe—as will be seen throughout—that a sex-typed
> subject is not so much involved as a format for constructing a picture.[42]

Florrie also displays the 'head cant', a further infantilizing technique
common in the 1970's advertisements collated and analysed by Goffman.
Florrie's head is lowered slightly, a posture described by Goffman as one
of 'acceptance of subordination, an expression of ingratiation, submissiveness, and appeasement'.[43] In contrast to the confident hand-on-hip
sexualized body display of Christine Dolce, Florrie is a coy modern
princess constructed to attract a young female 16–24 target age group.
Margerie Barbes-Petit, Brand Director for Parfums Nina Ricci, targeted
the young female consumer with a number of brand collaborations,
including Sony's Singstar game, to promote Florrie and allow consumers
the chance to 'compare themselves to the singer' by singing Sunday Girl,
the song from the TV advertisement. Consumers who gave the best
performances had a chance of winning *Nina* products and a Playstation 3
console and the event was promoted in stores as well as on social net-
working sites such as Facebook. 'Price is very important but consumers
are still looking for creativity and differentiation in their products and at
the point of sale. They can be seduced by a strong story and high perceived value,' explains Barbes-Petit. Samples of *Nina L'Elixir* were also
given out in cinema foyers during the showings of romcom films in a
further collaboration to target 16–24 year olds. The potent blend of consumerism, female-to-female comparison and celebrity aspiration that
characterizes Eve images in contemporary postfeminist advertising is not
limited only to the brand's promotional image, then; rather, it permeates
all areas of young women's lives and becomes a pervasive influence.

   A further common technique used in advertising is cropping the shot
to include or exclude certain body parts to bring the focus of the shot to
particular areas of the body.[44] Often cropping works to objectify and

42.   Goffman, *Gender Advertisements*, p. 45.
43.   Goffman, *Gender Advertisements*, p. 46.
44.   See G. Dyer, *Advertising as Communication* (London: Methuen, 1982); R. Coward,
Female Desire (London: Paladin, 1984); Jean Kilbourne, *Deadly Persuasion: Why Women
and Girls Must Fight the Addictive Power of Advertising* (New York: Free Press, 1999).

fetishize bodies, but where faces or eyes are cropped from the shot this technique can also function to dehumanize the person in the image.[45] For example, advertisements in which Eve is pictured with the serpent from Genesis 3 are usually more overtly sexual than those where she is pictured with the forbidden fruit. Furthermore, these images are usually unsuccessful at in any attempt to represent female sexual empowerment because of their use of cropping, which removes any sense of agency or self-empowerment through sexual objectification that could be attributed to Eve if these techniques were not employed. As I have argued above, the images of Eve with a red apple usually represent Eve as the ultimate agent provocateur. She is a postfeminist icon because she is, according to the advertisements, able to tempt others into doing what she wants because of her overwhelming desirability. In advertisements where Eve is pictured with only the snake, the postfeminist idea of empowerment through sexuality is undermined. The adverts are more concerned to display Eve's flesh and use the serpent as a phallic symbol than to present Eve as an empowered, sexually assertive individual (see, e.g. the advert for *Trussardi Python* perfume in Fig. 2.10). Significantly, the essential returned gaze of the female in postfeminist advertising, which is necessary to signify her empowerment, is almost always absent from these images.

Similarly the two brochure covers below (Figs. 3.14, 3.15) for Leeds Victoria Quarter's promotional magazine, *VQ*, and the clothing company, *Sisley*, further illustrate the disempowering effect of the absence of the female return gaze in postfeminist Eve advertising. Each cover features a representation of Eve with the serpent; however, both images have employed the sexist advertising technique of cropping the eyes from the head of the women, which objectifies and dehumanizes the women in the shot.[46] In the *VQ* advertisement, this technique is used to allow the consumer to see themselves as the tempting Eve, consuming to make herself even more desirable in the *VQ* garden of Eden. The *Sisley* shot, however, is aiming for the shock factor in the hope that young consumers will take notice of the brochure and then buy from it, since it is associating itself with sexuality and rebelliousness, themes that are attractive to its late-teen target consumers.

45. Cortese, *Provocateur*, p. 42.

46. This technique is traditionally almost always used on females in advertising except in postfeminist advertising when it is used on male bodies to objectify and sexualize them. See the discussion of images where Adam is depicted alone later in this chapter.

Figure 3.14. *Cover of* VQ *magazine* (*Leeds Victoria Quarter*),
Spring/Summer issue 2004

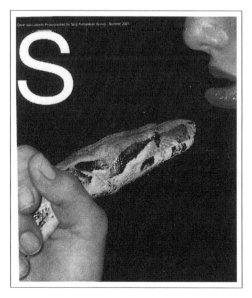

Figure 3.15. *Cover of* Sisley *brochure*, Lost in the Garden of Eden,
Spring/Summer issue 2001

Unlike the unisex brochures of *Sisley* and *VQ*, the Trussardi print advertisement appeared in a women's magazine. Interestingly, the perfume
did not sell well. Whether that is because postfeminist consumers picked
up on Eve's lack of agency in the image or it was simply a matter of
the perfume being unpleasant is not really the issue, since well-chosen
advertisements have always sold mediocre products to consumers. The
issue is that this advertisement highlights the fundamental weaknesses of
the postfeminist theme of female empowerment through self-objectification. The images are merely a recycling opportunity for traditional
patriarchally defined images of women in art produced in the nineteenth
century and in advertising produced in the 1970s. Postfeminist images
are packaging the traditional methods of women's negotiation tactics to
achieve power in patriarchal culture as a new form of feminism. In fact,
this kind of 'every woman for herself' survival tactic that women use in
societies defined by men is long established. For example, the form of
postfeminism sold in advertising today is remarkably similar to the
strategies of female sexual guile promoted by Helen Gurley Brown in her
1962 smash-hit bestseller, *Sex and the Single Girl: The Unmarried Woman's
Guide to Men.*[47] Brown's book was a self-help manual that provided
strategies for the modern single career girl of the time (who eventually
became the *Cosmo* girl) to rise above her limiting circumstances through
the tools of feminine transformation and sexual guile. Throughout the
sixties and on through the next few decades, Brown celebrated an exaggerated femininity that hinged upon the power to remake oneself into a
sexually desirable temptress. Brown summarizes the fundamental ideology
of what was to be seen by young women as female sexual empowerment
in postfeminist advertising over forty years later: 'Sex is a powerful
weapon for a single woman in getting what she wants from life'.[48]

The sexual strategic approach of Gurley Brown's *Sex and the Single Girl*
formed the template for the postfeminist empowerment through self-
objectification that we see in popular culture today.[49] Despite the overwhelming similarities between the Gurley Brown self-help guide and
postfeminist advertising ideology, a significant difference is that Gurley
Brown was advising women who did not have equality in any sense in

47.   Helen Gurley Brown, *Sex and the Single Girl: The Unmarried Woman's Guide to
Men* (New York: Open Road Iconic Books, 2012). Such was the popularity of this book
that it has been reprinted many times since its original release in 1962.

48.   Gurley Brown, *Sex and the Single Girl*, p. 7.

49.   Indeed Hurley's 1982 book, *Having it All: Love, Success, Sex, Money Even if
You're Starting with Nothing* (New York: Simon & Schuster, 1982), reads like an early
postfeminist manifesto.

society. The women who bought her book were women who felt they needed to transform themselves into sex objects to achieve any form of power in their lives. Gurley Brown's book, however, still proves relevant for a modern market. *Sex and the Single Girl* has already been reprinted twice since the turn of the century, along with its companion guidebook *Sex and the Office*.[50] Postfeminist advertising ideology, however, assumes that women enjoy equality in every area of their lives, ignoring the fact that this is not the experience of the women who subscribe to this brand of postfeminism. Advertising would not be successful at selling strategies for achieving female power if women already had it. As Jon Stratton comments in his study of the commodification of the body in advertising, *The Desirable Body*, 'turning men's desire for the female body to their own advantage…[is one] of the multiplicity of ways in which women today negotiate certain circumstances in their everyday lives'.[51] Following the lead of the Gurley Brown promotion of female sexuality as a way for women to achieve power, postfeminist sexual empowerment ideology, with its focus on the individual rather than the collective, does not offer any concrete solutions for obtaining equality, and only substitutes an autonomy based largely on sexual empowerment that is exclusive and dividing for women. Because postfeminism advertising ideology is concerned with selling products to women, the emphasis of the sexual empowerment they promote comes from exploring lifestyle choices and personal pleasures rather than outlining agendas for more direct and recognizable kinds of social activism. A recent advertising campaign for GHD hair straighteners demonstrates this point further.

GHD is the market-leading brand for hair straighteners, a position it has maintained through highly effective promotional campaigns that reverse traditional readings of myth and fairytale to promote the concepts of individual choice, female-to-female sexual competition and empowerment. GHD summarizes its brand ethos as 'the spirit of transformation'[52] and the advertising campaigns extend transformation to be as much about life transformation as hair. Since 2009 GHD have an ongoing campaign, Twisted Fairytales, in which well-known fairytales Rapunzel, Red Riding Hood and Cinderella get a postfeminist makeover—literally in the case of Cinderella—all with the strap-line 'You Can Do Anything with Your Hair'. In each advertisement it is the heroine's GHD-styled hair that is

50. Once in 2003 and once in 2012.

51. Jon Stratton, *The Desirable Body: Cultural Fetishism and the Erotics of Consumption* (Manchester: Manchester University Press, 1996), p. 239.

52. 'About GHD' on the official GHD website, http://www.ghdhair.com/about-ghd?PID=PRO-020&CRE=230&PLA=1 (accessed 21 December 2011).

the source of her empowerment. This series of advertisements follows the controversial *GHD: A New Religion for Hair* campaign, which focused on female sexual jealousy and competition with tag-lines such as, 'May my new curls make her feel choked with jealousy' and 'Make him dump her tonight and come home with me'. The campaign was banned after complaints from the Bishop of Liverpool and members of the public that the advertisements were offensive to the Christian faith.[53] The replacement Twisted Fairytales campaign maintained the equation of sexual attractiveness with sexual empowerment but focused more on empowerment through independence and personal choice than female sexual competition. In one image, for instance, an unsmiling Red Riding Hood stares back at the viewer, with an axe in one hand and in the other a basket with a wolf's tail poking out. The advertisement carries the rhyme:

> Little Red Riding Hood, neither timid nor shy
> While straightening her locks, a wolf she did spy
> But far from fainting or running a fever
> She started to laugh and pulled out a cleaver

More recently Eve has played a key role in advertising campaigns to communicate GHD's brand ethos of personal transformation through physical appearance and making the right consumer choice.

In 2010, for example, Eve imagery featured in the Choose Your Destiny campaign, an interactive 'tarot'-style website-based campaign in which consumers could choose their 'destiny' by the colour of their GHD straighteners. Choosing green meant choosing the personality of Eve, and choosing envy. In this campaign, as in postfeminist rhetoric more widely, that other women should be envious of your appearance and by extension your life, as symbolized by the consumer choice of GHD straighteners, is a desirable destiny to choose. In 2011 in a brand collaboration move similar to that of Nina Ricci's use of pop singer Florrie, GHD appointed pop singer Katy Perry as its 'brand ambassador'. Perry's fan base is huge and made up of young females in particular, and GHD can target its own market through Perry's worldwide tours, films and videos.[54] GHD's 2011 Christmas campaign continues the Snow White

---

53. See the ASA Adjudication on the campaign at http://www.asa.org.uk/ASA-action/Adjudications/2008/3/Jemella-Ltd/TF_ADJ_44122.aspx (accessed 26 August 2010), and Mark Sweney, 'Beauty Ad Banned after Christian Outcry', *The Guardian* (12 March 2008).

54. See GHD and Perry's brand tie-in events to target their crossover markets: 'GHD Katy Perry Tour Activation: Our Activation of Katy Perry's California Dreams tour delivered an amazing 51% Redemption for GHD', *Slice Experiential Marketing and Events*, http://slice.co.uk/about (accessed 21 December 2011).

theme but conflates the fairytale with Eve mythology. In the advertisement Perry is the innocent Snow White transformed, having bitten the poisonous apple/forbidden fruit, into a 1920's *femme fatale* siren. Again, colours are chosen carefully in the image to match the colour of the apple with the heels of Perry's shoes, her nails, lips and the GHD carrying case, linking sexiness with financial success and consumerism.

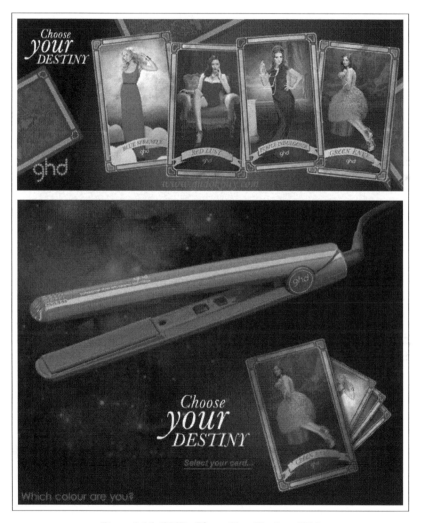

Figure 3.16. GHD, *Choose Your Destiny*, 2010

Figure 3.17. GHD, *Twisted Fairytales: Snow White*, 2011

Adam and Eve: A Happy Couple?

Advertisers use Adam and Eve as a paradigm for gender relations in contemporary society, reinscribing stereotypical notions of masculinity and femininity, and, because advertising in particular seeks to shape and influence consumer trends, they also use the biblical first couple to promote new ways for consumers to think about power dynamics in gender relations. This section focuses on the representation of Adam in advertising: How are we, as consumers, encouraged to view masculinity through images of Adam? Current representations of Adam appear to be a reversal of traditional gender display, showing men as the sum of their body parts in the same way that women have been displayed in advertising for decades. This book proposes that, rather than merely being symptomatic of the postfeminist condition, the images of an objectified Adam show up the contradictions in the concept of female empowerment through self-objectification. In most postfeminist discourse, men are in the background as objects of desire or villains, and this is no different in postfeminist Eve advertising where Adam is, quite often, a shadowy figure in the background. In an analysis of the images below, I argue that Adam is portrayed in this way to emphasize the message of postfeminist female empowerment promoted by the image of Eve as active, powerful agent in contrast to the passive, and apparently powerless, Adam.

In the previous chapters this book has illustrated how images of Eve have become increasingly popular in post-1990s popular culture as a vehicle to communicate notions about female and male sexuality for a postfeminist consumer. An image of Eve becomes visual shorthand for powerful female heterosexuality, sexuality that, if used correctly (i.e. if the correct products are consumed), will offer women a way of gaining the upper hand in contemporary gender relations. In these images, if Adam is portrayed at all, it is as an accessory, a 'himbo' with plenty of muscle but not too much brain. This objectification of Adam functions both to underscore the postfeminist notion of Eve as signifier for female sexual empowerment and undermine it by psychologically removing Adam from the episode of transgression. Although Adam is physically with Eve at the moment of transgression, by using licensed withdrawal the images suggest that psychologically he is not present. They thereby lay the responsibility for the transgression wholly at the feet of Eve. Adam's passivity contrasted with Eve's activity makes her appear powerful and in control, even dominant, in her role; however, repeating the notion that Eve was almost wholly responsible for the transgression in Genesis 2–3 does not so much suggest female empowerment as it perpetuates centuries of sexist stereotypes of women as sexual temptresses and reflects the lack of responsibility afforded to Adam in this episode in the biblical account in Genesis 2–3.

The images below, from two highly successful clothing companies, Versace and Benetton, are typical of contemporary portrayals of Adam and Eve. They represent Adam and Eve in similar ways: the couple are shown standing side by side, there is exposed flesh and Adam is depicted in a state of licensed withdrawal. The images are also highly sexually suggestive, although each provides a certain amount of calculated covering.

Figure 3.18. *Benetton advertisement, 1997*

Figure 3.19. *Versace Crockery advertisement,* Vogue, *August 1998*

In both pictures, Eve is the active figure. She gives the apple to Adam. Also in both pictures Eve looks at the camera with a knowing smile while Adam, expressionless, stares blankly either just above or just below the camera level. There are, however, subtle differences between the two, not in the way Eve is portrayed but in the way she is portrayed *vis-à-vis* Adam. In the Versace image Adam is hyper-masculinized and in the Benetton image he is feminized. These variations in the representation of Adam are significant because, while they treat Adam differently, they both indicate male power as a counter-balance to the female sexual power being promoted in the images. In the case of the Versace image the male power being suggested by the hyper-masculinized physique of Sylvester Stallone is that of physical strength and dominance. In the Benetton image the androgynous representation of Adam coupled with the sacred heart symbolism of the apple transforms Adam from passive, powerless himbo to a Christ-figure redeeming the temptress Eve.

First of all, to illustrate the function of Adam's hyper-masculinity in the Versace advertisement it is necessary to engage with another one of Goffman's observations on gender representation in advertising from his seminal 1976 study. Here, Goffman uses the concept of relative size to describe the way advertisers use the advantage of height as a visual indication of power and authority. A taller figure in an advertisement has greater power and authority than figures shorter than he or she is, and a figure positioned higher than others, regardless of the figures' relative heights, also has the greater authority.[55] Characteristically it is men who are positioned above women in ads. On occasions when women are shown as relatively larger, or are positioned higher than men, they also have a higher social status than those men. Even though the relative size shows the woman's status advantage in the Versace advertisement above, this advantage is illusory because the male in the image shows an alternative and more significant power. Adam is hyper-masculinized: he is portrayed as athletic and strong. He stands in the pose of a weight-lifter or sportsman, showing his heavily muscled physique off to its best advantage. While Eve may have the relative size advantage in terms of height, there is no doubt that Adam has the relative size advantage in terms of width and potential physical power. The viewer understands that though Eve may have the higher status in this scenario, Adam could easily physically dominate her if he wished.

Significantly, Adam does not look at the viewer, or even at the apple being offered to him by Eve, but stares into the distance, appearing to be psychologically removed from the scenario. This effect not only lessens the apparent threat of physical force on his part but removes responsibility from Adam. Goffman also uses the concept of function ranking to

---

55. For instance, in advertisements portraying a family, the head of that family would never be presented as sitting or kneeling while other, lower status members of the family stand. See Goffman, *Gender Advertisements*, p. 37.

describe a particular structure of gender inequality in which the male model in an ad performs the important role while the female model occupies a less meaningful role. In the two advertisements reproduced here, the opposite is the case: Eve performs the important role while Adam is in licensed withdrawal, representing a lower social status in what Goffman refers to as the 'hierarchy of functions'.[56]

In advertising criticism the gender differences evident in the way that hands are shown is known as 'feminine touch' and 'masculine grip' because women are often portrayed as touching or caressing themselves, whereas men are portrayed as gripping. The Versace ad goes beyond the Benetton ad in subverting traditional sexist practices in advertising by depicting Adam touching his legs. Eve's hands and arms, in contrast, remain totally out of contact with any other part of her body.[57] What is the point in this subversion? What message are these ads communicating to the consumer? In being active, engaged with the spectator and, because the man is passive, being responsible for the man's welfare, Eve assumes the lion's share of responsibility and blame for what happens. Of course, the reason advertisers recycle the story in Genesis 2–3 so frequently is because everyone knows what happens: Eve leads Adam into temptation and brings about his ruin. The vast majority of people in Western society are familiar with the biblical story and most likely, and most importantly, the consumers targeted by these advertisements will know the story in this its culturally appropriated form.

In these advertisements the traditional advertising techniques that are used for men are used for women and vice versa. In the Benetton ad this gender spin results in the man being feminized; he sports long hair and he is not altogether physically different from Eve. In the Versace ad, however, the gender spin does not feminize Adam. In casting the hyper-feminine Claudia Schiffer as Eve, and the hyper-masculine Sylvester Stallone as Adam, the advertisers ensure that Adam cannot possibly look feminine. Although he has taken on the traditional female charac-teristics in advertising, the feminine touch and licensed withdrawal, Stallone's masculinity is defined in opposition to Schiffer's femininity.

56. Goffman, *Gender Advertisements*, p. 32.

57. The position of her legs, however, betray the advertisement's adherence to strict rules of gender postures: Eve's legs are touching, in what seems to be a modest gesture, and is most certainly a feminine one. Also, she displays what Goffman refers to as the 'bashful knee bend', a posture frequently taken by women in advertising, but rarely by men, that 'can be read as an acceptance of subordination, an expression of ingratiation, submissiveness, and appeasement', showing that the representation of Eve's empower-ment through the subversion of traditional gendered advertising techniques is not entirely successful. See Goffman, *Gender Advertisements*, p. 169.

Stallone is muscular, Schiffer is smooth; Stallone is dark, Schiffer is fair. Even the height difference works in favour of these opposites: Schiffer is tall and lithe; Stallone is stocky and powerful. In recreating physical gender ideals instead of subverting them, Versace ensures that its advertisement comforts rather than disturbs the consumer. The advertisers are not interested in undermining anything traditional; rather, they are interested in persuading the consumer to find Versace sexy. Even Benetton, notorious for its attempts to disturb the consumer, does not do much to undermine any traditional gender characteristics or Eve stereotypes. Their Eve is portrayed as sexual. Whereas Adam's jeans are buttoned, hers are undone and partially unzipped. The denim jacket she wears is left open, exposing almost all of one breast, and a serpent hangs around her neck, alluding to the serpent in the garden story, thereby reinscribing notions of highly sexualized, deceptive and seductive femininity.

The Benetton image is more than just an image of Adam and Eve where Adam is in his usual state of licensed withdrawal and Eve is displaying her powers of attraction. Adam in this image is also Jesus, the second Adam, the Adam who redeems the sins of the world. Eve, however, is still Eve the sinner. Adam's feminization in this image becomes clear when his role as Jesus also becomes clear. As Jesus, he is not threatened by the temptress and does not need to be hyper-masculinized to compensate for his lack of power in the image.

Figure 3.20. *Print advertisement for Korn jeans, 2001*

Similarly, the advertisement for jeans in Figure 3.20 has also made the link between Adam and Jesus. These advertisements highlight the fundamental difference between Adam taking the fruit and Eve giving it: when Eve is giving the fruit she is giving sin, when Adam takes the fruit he is taking away the sin. While Eve is constant in her role as sexual temptress, Adam is either not held responsible for the transgression episode or he is the redeemer of Eve. This difference in the gender roles of the man and the woman show the serious imbalance between the ways that women and men are perceived in popular culture. On deeper analysis these advertisements do not subvert traditional attitudes to gender but simply recycle them.

Figure 3.21. *Print advertisement from German magazine, 2000*

All the advertisements showing Adam and Eve together that I have found during my research for this book follow this pattern of representation. Adam is either portrayed as a background figure, barely visible against the fore-grounded sexuality of Eve, is pictured in a state of licensed withdrawal or is given the role of redeemer to Eve's sinner. A further technique to reduce Adam's responsibility in the transgression scene and emphasize Eve's powers of attraction is the portrayal of Adam as so taken by the overwhelming desirability of Eve that he will do anything she wants. For instance, in Figure 3.21 the advertisers use the relative size technique to suggest Eve's dominance over Adam.[58] Eve offers him the forbidden fruit but he is in no position to resist. He is well and truly beneath her, having to reach to take the fruit. Typically, he is so overwhelmed by the sexual desirability of Eve, he is not responsible for his actions. For this reason, Adam is often pictured as engrossed in a part of Eve's body.

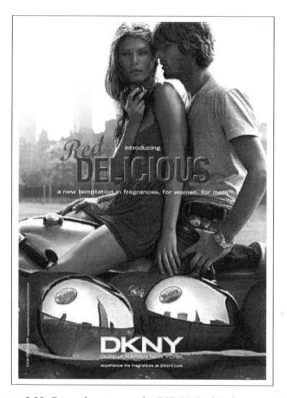

Figure 3.22. *Print advertisement for DKNY,* Red Delicious, *2005*

In Figure 3.22 Adam finds Eve so desirable that he cannot take his eyes from her, despite the fact that she does not return his ardour. In true postfeminist advertising style, she returns the viewer's gaze instead of Adam's. She wears a red mini-dress, which shows her bare thighs and also connects her with the apple she is eating and the fragrance she is, presumably, wearing to get such a strong response from Adam. The fragrance in the foreground is the shape and colour of advertising's traditional forbidden fruit: the red apple. Once again, the red apple signifies

58. Unfortunately I have lost the reference.

female sexuality and desirability. The advertisement tells the viewer that
if she wears this perfume she will have the same effect on men as the
model in the image. Eve's empowerment is signified not only by the
dramatic effect she has had on Adam but also by the fact that he sits
behind on her on the motorbike, a vehicle usually associated with men.
Women, if they do ride them, tend to be the passenger. Eve is in charge
in this image, empowered by her sexuality. She sits at the front of the
motorbike, besotted man behind her, while she eats the fruit that
connotes individual choice and empowerment in postfeminist advertising. To further cement the associations between the fragrance and
postfeminist empowerment, the background of the image shows the
Manhattan skyline, made famous to the target consumers of the fragrance
and the readers of *InStyle* magazine[59] by the most popular postfeminist
television show, *Sex and the City*. The by-line to the image says 'a new
temptation in fragrances, for women, for men'. The copy associates the
fragrance not only with the forbidden fruit and the woman but by adding
'for men' to the end of the by-line, the advertisement makes clear that
the fragrance is being sold as a tool for women to attract men.

Even the reality programme *Expedition Robinson* has employed Eve
imagery to promote the series.[60] The advertisement, which promotes the
start of the 1999 series, tries to attract the interest of potential viewers by
using a naked Adam and Eve as the promotional bait. Links are drawn
between the paradisal Malaysian island in which the programme is set
and the garden of Eden. *Expedition Robinson* is a reality game-show in
which contestants have to survive life on a tropical island by means of
guile, deception, inventiveness and intelligence. The advertisers clearly
thought Eve, wearing a particularly ruthless expression in this image,
would be the ideal symbol to attract an audience, suggesting to viewers of
the programme that they would be tuning in to watch contestants use sex
and the display of female sexuality as a means to win the series. Adam,
on the other hand, is given no credit for guile. He is pictured in licensed
withdrawal, expressionlessly gazing in the direction of the snake and
Eve's naked breasts, while Eve dreams of being a contestant on *Expedition
Robinson*.

59. *InStyle* magazine targets 18–25-year-old females and consists solely of articles
and photographic stories that centre on appearance. The magazine focuses on emulating
celebrity style and the promotion of designer goods.

60. Known as *Survivor* in the UK.

Figure 3.23. *Print advertisement for* Expedition Robinson
reality show (German Version), 1999

Expedition Robinson has not been the only reality competition series that sets women contestants against each other for the opportunity to win a valuable prize. *America's Next Top Model*, hosted by the supermodel and chat-show host Tyra Banks, is a popular American series (but also shown across Europe) to find the next supermodel. Eleven finalists are put through a series of modelling assignments, with the contestant who is considered by the judges to have done the worst in the task being sent home each week.

The show is the ultimate example of the difficulties of postfeminist empowerment through sexuality and self-objectification. The eleven women are all young, beautiful and desperate for success. They want this success to come through the route of their sexuality, using Tyra Banks (the show's host and a former supermodel who was also included in Forbes's Celebrity 100 list in 2007) as their mentor. Banks has achieved power and wealth through self-objectification, but, as the by-line for the show's promotional image says, 'They're all gorgeous. But only one has got what it takes to be…America's Next Top Model.' The show sums up the nature of postfeminist empowerment through self-objectification: it is an exclusive enterprise—although many women may compete with each other, only very few can succeed in achieving any power through self-objectification.

The first show of the 2004 season saw the eleven contestants modelling in an advertising campaign for Freshlook coloured contact lenses. The theme of the campaign was the temptation scene in Genesis 3. Each contestant modelled a shot as Eve, and Eve's representation changed with each contestant, depending on their ethnic origin, complexion or 'type of look'. Eve's theme was changed for each contestant to reflect the way the coloured contact lenses can give the same person a different look each time they are used. Each woman was naked except for body-paint, and often the serpent, and occasionally the forbidden fruit (apple), was painted onto the model's body. The common themes in all the shots are self-display and the foregrounding of female sexuality as a means to achieve power. The women objectify their bodies and display them as sites of sexual temptation to win votes from judges who decide which woman is the most desirable. Adam is always in the background of the image, being, quite literally, kept in the dark by the advertisers. He functions as a symbol of the status and desirability of Eve. In each shot he takes a position of subjugation, kneeling, sitting or lying by Eve, but always staring at her in awe.

April, the contestant represented as 'Asian Eve', has the serpent (represented as a Chinese dragon) painted onto her body. The apple is painted onto the fan she is holding. She faces the viewer; the tempting display is for them despite the fact that Adam stands in the background, a dark shadow looking on. Once again, the advertising campaign follows the biblical text by including Adam at the transgression scene but as a secondary character in the scene, while Eve is foregrounded.

Figure 3.24. *Asian Eve*

The second image (Fig. 3.25) of the campaign presents the contestant as Caribbean Eve because of her Afro-Caribbean ethnicity. Here, Eve is represented as a peacock, often a symbol of vanity, tempting the viewer with her bright and varied plumage. She holds aloft a large exotic red fruit, while Adam, again shadowy at the right side of the picture, kneels and reaches his hand to the fruit. Eve does not so much tempt Adam with the fruit as goad him with it, holding it high where he cannot reach it and ignoring him in favour of the viewer, who will judge her desirability.

The third image depicts Catie as 'Heavenly Eve' (Fig. 3.26). She is an angel, whose serpent functions as a headband. Once again she is positioned for the viewer, with whom she makes eye contact. Although Adam, again lurking in the background, gazes in awe, the apple is not held within his reach; the apples are merely symbolic of the contestant's desirability and empowerment through her self-objectification.

Figure 3.25. *Caribbean Eve*

Figure 3.26. *Heavenly Eve*

Figure 3.27. *Floral Eve*

Figure 3.28. *Enchanting Archer Eve*

The next contestant, Heather (Fig. 3.27), is represented as 'Floral Eve'. She holds a red apple fashioned from flowers. Just like all the other Eves in the campaign, she returns the viewer's gaze. The apple is offered to the viewer as much as it is offered to Adam, who kneels at her side.

The fourth image (Fig. 3.28) is entitled 'Enchanting Archer Eve' because the contestant, Jenascia, is representing Eve as an archer. A play on cupid, Archer Eve's body is painted red; she has large red-feathered wings clipped to her back and an enormous hat that looks like it is fashioned out of large petals and leaves. She has flowers attached to her chest, and red gloves cover her hands and arms. The obligatory red apple is painted onto the end of the arrow. Adam is again kneeling in front of her, staring at her. But Eve looks at us, the viewers. Indeed, the arrow is not aimed at Adam, it is aimed at the judge of her desirability, the viewer.

Figure 3.29. *Egyptian Eve*

Returning to the theme of basing the contestant's representation of Eve on their ethnic origin, Mercedes is dressed as 'Egyptian Eve' (Fig. 3.29). A snake is painted slithering up her leg and a further snake is painted onto her shawl. Adam sits in the background, staring up at the towering Eve. She holds a large red apple in her left hand—nowhere near Adam—and although her lower body is turned towards Adam, she twists the top half of her body to display it for the viewer, whom she faces, returning their gaze.

Figure 3.30. *Medieval Eve*

Sara, who features in the campaign as 'Medieval Eve' (Fig. 3.30), is painted silver and dressed as a half-naked knight in chain-mail head-wear. She is the only one of the Eves in the full series of shots who is engaged in physical contact with Adam. He is in the shadow and kneels before her, holding her leg, while she has one finger in his mouth. This display of sexually suggestive body language is purely for the viewer, however, for it is the viewer she looks at and it is to the viewer she is offering the chain-mail apple.

The image below (Fig. 3.31) presents Shandi as 'Lady Godiva Eve'. Like her namesake, this Eve is naked except for the hair extensions and the long hair painted onto her body. She turns her back to Adam to display her body to the viewer better, and, although she is holding the apple in Adam's direction, it is as much directed at the viewer with whom she is really engaged as she returns the their gaze.

Figure 3.31. *Lady Godiva Eve*

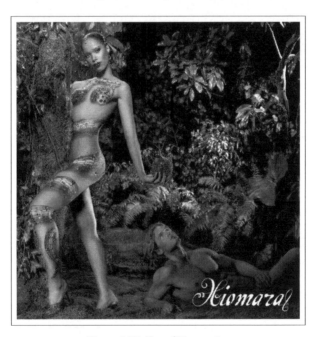

Figure 3.32. *Eve of Temptation*

Hiomara's representation of Eve involves only the theme of temptation—hence her shot is titled 'Eve of Temptation' (Fig. 3.32). She holds
the apple towards Adam, who lies on the ground looking up at Eve. The
snake is painted as entwined around Eve's body with another red apple in
its mouth. Once again Eve's naked body is displayed for the viewer and
she returns their gaze.

Bethany's representation of Eve is titled 'Eve of Winter' (Fig. 3.33)
and her body is painted blue. She wears a blue and white wig and the
apple is made of ice. Adam is lying down to the left of Eve and, although
she holds the apple in his direction, its position is far too high for him to
reach nor does he make a movement to reach it. Eve's naked body, as
usual in this campaign, is displayed for the viewer, with whom she makes
eye contact.

Figure 3.33. *Eve of Winter*

The final image of the Eve series shows the contestant Yoanna presented
as 'Eve of the Night' (Fig. 3.34). Her naked body is painted shocking
pink and she holds a crescent moon accessory, which holds the apple.
This is only image in the series in which Adam is not looking at Eve. He
maintains his position of subjugation by sitting on the ground close to
Eve, half-standing, half-kneeling, but, instead of gazing at Eve in awe,
encouraging the viewer recognize her overwhelming desirability and do
the same, in this shot Adam looks off camera to the left while Eve
matches the viewers' gaze with hers.

Figure 3.34. *Eve of the Night*

This *Fresh Look* advertising campaign is rarely successful in representing
the contestants as desirable and sexually empowered women. Although
the images use many of the representational techniques outlined by
Goffman to convey Eve's power, status and desirability, the fundamental
flaw of the campaign is that it makes Eve look ridiculous rather than
sexy, desirable and empowered. Adam's darkly lit background presence in
each image signifies the women's higher social status and her power over
him. In many of the images he kneels before her, as she towers majesti-
cally above him in four-inch stiletto heels. She is the active participant
in the scene; she offers the apple and matches the viewers' gaze with hers.
Eve's self-objectification, however, does not convey any sense of empowerment to the viewer because these women appear naked apart from
ridiculous accessories. To be adult females dressed as 'Enchanting Archer
Eve', or 'Heavenly Eve' painted blue with images of cherubs on her chest
does not suggest the empowerment of these women but their disempowerment. They are made to look vain, child-like and ridiculous in the
campaign, despite all the techniques, such as the function of Adam,
employed to suggest otherwise. As this book has argued, postfeminist
advertising depoliticizes and domesticates feminism by reducing real
women's experience of inequality to the single issue of achieving power
through sexuality. This advertising campaign exposes the inanity of
attempting to achieve power through being judged on appearance and

market value. Significantly, the contestant who refused to participate in the campaign was the one who was expelled from the competition that week.

It Is Not Good that the Man Should Be Alone

This section will look at images of Adam that treat the male body in similar ways as the female body has traditionally been treated in advertising; for example, images in which Adam is treated as a 'sex object' and techniques traditionally reserved for the objectified female body are used to display the male sexualized body. In Figure 3.35, for instance, part of the Leeds *VQ* advertising campaign in August 2004, the display techniques of cropping, objectification and fetishization are applied to the male body. Cropping so that a body part is separated from the rest of the body creates a dehumanising effect and results in the fetishization of that body part. The representation of Adam's body seems to indicate

Figure 3.35. *Promotional flyer for Leeds Victoria Quarter, August 2004*

a certain equality or rebalance in the display of the genders: women may be on exhibit as sexual objects but all is equal because men receive the same treatment. However, as I argued in the last section of this chapter, the 'meanings' and connotations inherent in the representation of female and male naked bodies are significantly different. What Margaret R. Miles argues about nakedness in the art of the Christian West applies here:

> Female nakedness is presented as a symbol of sin, sexual lust, and dangerous evil. In depictions of the naked female body interest in active religious engagement, exercise, and struggle is often subordinated to, or in tension with, the female spectacle.[61]

61. Miles, *Carnal Knowing*, p. 81.

> Since antiquity male nakedness has been used to represent 'physical strength as
> a symbol of extraordinary spiritual strength'. Heroic struggle against tempta-
> tion, sense of personal choice, and single-minded, undistracted pursuit of an
> athletic crown characterized spiritual 'atheletes'. Male nakedness represented
> spiritual discipline and physical control and order.[62]

Inherent in the images that some advertising critics have termed 'beef-
cake himbos'[63] is the promise of power, power that is represented by the
over-developed and clearly physically strong male torsos (and notice that
unlike the images of women in advertising where almost any body part
can be cropped and fetishized and can stand for sexuality these com-
parable images of men tend to focus on the torso). These portrayals of
masculinity may at first appear to be an attempt to show the vulnerability
of males to the power of female sexuality, or, as with the VQ advert
below, to show a more 'sensitive male' by diluting the effect of the physically powerful torso by feminising the image with flowers and traditionally feminine decoration. Actually, however, they perpetuate traditional
gender ideals, and, in fact, the gender codes in the text, through their
emphasis on the physical strength of the male body.

The advertising critic Anthony Cortese argues that the recent trend
in the objectification of the male body is in itself is a reaction to postfeminist culture. He comments that a physically powerful look validates
masculine identity and provides a dominating image for safety and
protection. Furthermore, he argues, the strong physical image of men in
postfeminist advertising allows advertisers to target the whole range of
male consumers, since muscularity and strength are highly valued within
the male sports subculture by men of all races and social classes.[64] This
image of the male body is becoming more prevalent in contemporary
advertising as a reaction to compensate for an increase in women's
economic, political and social power. Advertisers reconceptualize images
of men as they lose control over the ability to influence their wives,
girlfriends, mothers or sisters. The hyper-masculine physique is suggestive
of physical intimidation. If men can no longer dominate women eco-
nomically, politically and socially, in advertising their bodies become
overdeveloped to appear much bigger and stronger than women's so that
physical domination is implied.[65]

62. Miles, *Carnal Knowing*, p. 142.
63. See Cortese, *Provocateur*, pp. 58-62; Sammy R. Danna, 'Sexier and More
Sensitive: The Changing Advertising Image of Males in the 1990s', in Luigi Manca and
Alessandra Manca (eds.), *Gender and Utopia in Advertising: A Critical Reader* (Lisle, IL:
Propcopian Press, 1994), pp. 73-86.
64. Cortese, *Provocateur*, pp. 58-62.
65. Cortese, *Provocateur*, p. 60.

The Adam images prevalent in contemporary advertising may be a new thing, they may be reaction to, or reflection of, contemporary postfeminist social and cultural notions. But there is more to it than this. If we look at the origins of the image, at the state of gender relations in the text that the image is adapting, then the function of Adam's objectified body becomes clearer. His passivity in the text is translated by the advertisers into his 'himbo' image—a man who is physically strong but mentally weak. The images of Adam problematize the concept of female sexual power as exemplified in postfeminist advertising because they imply that females have sexual desire too. If one can become powerful or weaker through sexual desire, then Eve must be as vulnerable as Adam to the loss of power through sexual desire. Such a loss of power through sexual desire is, as I argued in Chapter 2, implied in the biblical text, and it is assumed in popular culture versions of the story.

In depicting Adam and Eve, the advertiser is able to convey a whole range of complex concepts and selling points to a carefully targeted audience using a single image. Representations of male and female nakedness in Western culture are saturated with meaning, and male and female nakedness signify different qualities and concepts to the viewer. The body is the site of rich visual symbolism and female and male nakedness are heavily invested with social and religious meaning. By representing Adam in advertising, marketers can sell an idealized image of masculinity that carries political implications. In the same way that popular cultural images of Eve can represent a postfeminist view of femininity, where the female is an active agent, powerful in her highly sexualized, fetishized form, Adam enables advertisers to portray a postfeminist view of masculinity, where the male may be passive, but nevertheless embody physical strength and power. These images of Adam convey an underlying theme of ability to dominate through superior strength. In both types of representation, the body is the locus of power. Marketing images of Adam and Eve allow us to see how advertising, the most influential institution in popular culture, represents the problematic gender relations experienced in postfeminist Western society.

Moreover, in the postfeminist social climate, men are becoming increasingly objectified in advertising because it is an unusual and, for the consumer, unexpected change of tactic. The advertiser gives the postfeminist consumer a knowing wink when it portrays a muscle-bound male as a sex object. It is the insertion of men into the traditional role of women as provocateur, as Cortese puts it, and it is good business. Images such as Figure 3.35, the image of Adam's cropped torso advertising Leeds Victoria Quarter, target both male and female consumers.

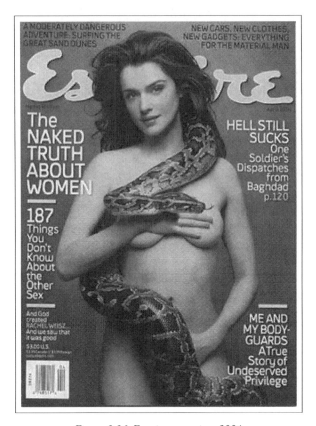

Figure 3.36. Esquire *magazine, 2004*

Muscularity as masculinity is a motif in ads that target upper-income men as well as those in the lower range of social stratification. Advertisers often use representations of physically rugged or muscular male bodies to masculinize goods and services aimed at elite male consumers. This form of advertising to the male market does just what adverts of Eve do for female consumers: encourage them to buy a product or patronize a shopping venue by selling a prescriptive and unrealistic body image and the encoded gender messages that those idealized body images communicate to the viewer. Interestingly enough, images of Eve are rarely cropped to show only a torso without a head. As this chapter has illustrated, the occasions when her image is cropped are images that are sold to the male glamour magazine market or when the postfeminist message is either undermined or not present. Eve is more likely to be found with various props and, rather than physical power or strength as is the case with Adam, the site of Eve's power is her sexuality. She is more likely to be

portrayed in a semi-pornographic pose with a python as the *Esquire* cover
(Fig. 3.36) illustrates. Eve is all about sex. Her power is her sexuality. Her
relationship with the serpent is sexual. The forbidden fruit that she offers
to the viewer is her sexuality, her power. Compare the image of Eve here
with the one of Adam that follows (Fig. 3.37).

Figure 3.37. *Print advertisement for Mey underwear, 2000*

Figure 3.37 shows the hyper-masculinized Adam. He is muscular,
athletic-looking and he is in licensed withdrawal. In fact, the audience
can barely see his face, which is in shadow. This refusal to return the
viewer's gaze is common in advertising images where a man is objectified.
Adam is displayed as a sexual object, appealing to both heterosexual and
homosexual consumers. The significant thing is that Adam does not raise
his eyes to the viewer, he does not accept his role as a sexual object in
the way that he does in images where Eve is pictured alone. Both Brian
Pronger and Kenneth MacKinnon, critics of popular cultural images of
men, agree that the vast majority of contemporary images where the male
is made a sex object include a disavowal of the male gaze.[66] While the
advertisements may attract a gay male consumer the man in the image
does not risk putting off heterosexual male consumers by returning the
gay male gaze. This technique offers advertisers a wide-ranging consumer

66.   See Kenneth MacKinnon, *Uneasy Pleasures: The Male as Erotic Object* (London:
Cygnus Arts, 1997); Brian Pronger, *The Arena of Masculinity: Sports, Homosexuality and
the Meaning of Sex* (London: Gay Men's Press, 1994).

appeal and manages to appeal to the gay market, a market notoriously difficult for advertisers to harness.[67] Advertisers must tread a fine line because they have to try not to alienate the heterosexual market while simultaneously reaching out to the homosexual market. As in the Versace advert, usually in Adam and Eve advertisements where the couple are pictured together, the homoerotic implications of this representation are kept at bay by the presence of Eve. In advertisements where Adam is pictured alone he must deflect the homoerotic implications of his representation by appearing in licensed withdrawal: just as he has no responsibility in the transgression episode, he has no responsibility for his objectification. At present, advertisers seem to agree with God in Genesis 2 that it is not good that the man should be alone.

67. The gay male market is an extremely valuable market sector for advertisers because on average gay men have a greater disposable income than the rest of the general population.

4

FORBIDDEN FRUIT TASTES THE SWEETEST: EVE IMAGERY IN ADVERTISING FOR THE *DESPERATE HOUSEWIVES* FRANCHISE

One of the most successful TV franchises of all time is the US comedy-drama series *Desperate Housewives*. The series began in October 2004 on the ABC network in the US and since then has become the most popular show for 18–49 year old females worldwide, sold to fifty countries globally, with an audience of approximately 119 million viewers. The opening credits of the series feature Adam and Eve and the red apple forbidden fruit motif, which became the show's merchandising and promotional motif as the series grew in popularity and consumer pulling power.

This chapter will look at the ways that the *Desperate Housewives* TV franchise employed Eve imagery in promotional material to promote successfully a postfeminist politik of consumer choice and power to a predominantly female audience, despite the more complex constructions of gender and female sexuality in the series. Advertising for *Desperate Housewives* exploited the forbidden fruit symbolism already embedded in the psyche of the female fan base of the franchise. The postfeminist link between desirability, temptation, individual choice and consumerism featured heavily in the campaign, to the point that a perfume bearing the name *Forbidden Fruit* was launched.[1]

---

1. There are striking parallels here with the phenomenally successful *Twilight* film franchise. The opening film in the franchise, based on Stephanie Meyer's best-selling vampire-themed fantasy romance novels, grossed $35.7 million on its opening day, and grossed $408.9 million worldwide. The DVD, released on 21 March 2009, became one of the top selling DVDs of that year, grossing an additional $181 million in sales. Such was the popularity of the *Twilight* saga in film and in print that it spawned a whole merchandising range, from clothing to cosmetics to jewellery. The most popular image of 2008 had to be the red apple forbidden fruit that graced the cover of the *Twilight* novel and was featured in almost every *Twilight* advertisement and merchandising product.

Notably, the *Twilight* franchise also launched a perfume bearing the name *Forbidden Fruit*. The difference between the two promotional campaigns is that where *Twilight*

Desperate Housewives centres on the lives of five main female characters and how they negotiate their friendships, relationships, marriages,
families and jobs, while uncovering and hiding secrets along the way.
The postfeminist tenet of promoting individual choice is one of the basic
themes of the show. Marc Cherry, the creator of the show, told *Newsweek* during an interview that, when developing *Desperate Housewives*, he
'wanted to write something about choices we make in life and what
happens when that does not go well. All the women have made some
kind of choice in their life and are in various stages of regretting it. That
is where the desperation comes from.'[2]

Cherry hit on a concept that resonated with millions of viewers
(mostly female) all over the Western world. The primetime comedy-
drama series takes a darkly comedic look at suburbia, where the secret
lives of housewives are not always what they seem. The series began with
Mary Alice Young (Brenda Strong) leaving her perfect house in the love-
liest of suburbs to commit suicide. She then narrates the whole series,
taking the viewer into the lives of her family, friends and neighbours.
Her circle of girlfriends on Wisteria Lane include Susan Mayer (Teri
Hatcher), the divorcee and single mother who will go to extraordinary
lengths for love; Lynette Scavo (Felicity Huffman), who struggles with
balancing the complications of work and family issues; Bree Van de Kamp
(Marcia Cross) who battles the demons of widowhood, alcoholism and
vengeful children; Gabrielle Solis (Eva Longoria), the beautiful trophy
wife who accepts jewellery from her husband in exchange for sex and
conducts an affair with her young male gardener; and serial divorcee
Edie Britt (Nicolette Sheridan), the real estate maven whose colourful
love-life and vindictive personality keep the neighbourhood buzzing.
From the show's opening credits, the private lives (as opposed to the
façade of domestic contentment that the women try to maintain) of the
main female characters are connected with the temptation scene in
Genesis 3. The credits contain references to famous pieces of art, which
portray domesticity through the ages. The first image is a copy of the
painting *Adam and Eve* by Lucas Cranach the Elder (Fig. 4.0).

markets heterosexual romance, pre-marital sexual abstention and monogamy as desirable choices for young female consumers (while ensuring that the same consumers
look as sexually attractive as possible with the help of the *Twilight* cosmetics range), the
Desperate Housewives promotional campaigns present the series as a dark sexy comedy
about contemporary women's complex lifestyle choices, a complexity that is undermined
by the series promotional campaigns which sell 'ironic' constructions of femininity
through the lead actresses.

2. Interview with Marc Cherry, *Newsweek*, October 2005.

Figure 4.0. *Lucas Cranach the Elder,* Adam and Eve, *1526*

A snake passes an apple to Eve before another larger apple, with the words '*Desperate Housewives*' written on it, falls on Adam.

Figure 4.1. *Title credits,* Desperate Housewives, ABC *Network*

At the end of the credits, the tree of the knowledge of good and evil appears again, this time with a snake wrapped around a branch, and the four main characters, Bree, Lynette, Susan and Gabriel, all appear under the tree and catch a falling apple.

Figure 4.2. *Title credits*, Desperate Housewives, *ABC Network*

The *Adam and Eve* painting and the image of the five woman holding apples is a reference to individual choice—the choices that the women make and the ways they must then negotiate the needs and desires in their lives as a consequence of those choices. For instance, Lynette had to choose motherhood over career but deeply resents her position as stay-at-home mum as well as her husband, who enjoys a greater freedom because he is not expected to be equally involved in child-care and domestic duties. The ex-model, Gabriella, has chosen to marry her husband and commit herself to being a trophy wife in return for financial security. Despite her choice to marry for money, Gabriella is not happy with her husband and is having an affair with the teenage gardener. Each woman is involved in various lies, deceits or scandals at any one time during the show and the apple in the credits also signifies the women's cunning and deviousness in these daily negotiations, playing on attributes traditionally ascribed to Eve in Genesis 3.

The explosive success of the series has spawned mass apple-related *Desperate Housewives* merchandizing to exploit the market potential of the show's popularity, including clothing (most notably a T-shirt with an image of a red apple on the front, emblazoned with the words, 'It's time to come clean', referring to the many secrets of the women of Wisteria

Lane), games, books, a *Desperate Housewives* Cookbook (with the tag-line: 'Juicy Dishes and Saucy Bits')[3] and the new *Forbidden Fruit* fragrance, which will be discussed later in this chapter. The red apple theme has been continued through all the promotional images and merchandising that have been produced by the show, usually using images that connect the female character of the show with the concepts signified by the apple and, of course, Eve: individual choice, deception, temptation, sin and desirability.

There are three main examples of the show employing Eve imagery to sell its products, all of which appeared around the time of the start of the second series of *Desperate Housewives* in 2005. The first example is a print advertisement, featuring Eva Longoria as Eve, which promotes the second season of the show to its German audience; the second is the second-season promotional trailer featuring the theme 'Juicy'; and the third example is the print advertisement for the *Desperate Housewives: Forbidden Fruit* fragrance. By the end of the first season *Desperate Housewives* had enjoyed overwhelming success and popularity, especially among the female audience age range 18–34. Two of its stars in particular, Teri Hatcher and Eva Longoria, had become celebrity staples of women's popular magazines that also target this age group. Longoria had by now won a lucrative contract with L'Oreal, a company that also appeals to the same market as magazines for the young female consumer and the same market sector as the *Desperate Housewives* show.

The new promotional material for the show reflected Hatcher and Longoria's status as popular, desirable, successful female celebrities. Longoria in particular was singled out among the stars of *Desperate Housewives* to advertise the upcoming season to the German market. She also starred in the most sensual scene in the second season TV trailer.

The print advertisement to promote the show's new season to the German audience featured an image of Longoria holding a red apple. She returns the viewer's gaze and smiles. The red apple reflects the promotional material of the show and its opening credits; however, the picture is also typical of a postfeminist Eve advertising image. Longoria courts the viewer by tempting them to watch the show with her desirability— the viewers are enticed to watch the show to see more of her.

---

3. Christopher Style and Scott S. Tobis, *The 'Desperate Housewives' Cookbook: Juicy Dishes and Saucy Bits* (New York: Hyperion, 2006).

Figure 4.3. Desperate Housewives,
StarForce Channel TV advertisement, August 2005

Figure 4.4. Desperate Housewives, *German print advertisement, 2005*

The use of postfeminist advertising images in the show's promotional material is not surprising, since the series offers postfeminism as packaged entertainment to its wide audience share. In each episode, as various tragedies, dramas and events unfold around the characters, the show suggests that the women are not victims of the circumstances or developments in their lives because, as Debbie Rodan proposes in her critique of the use of postfeminism in *Desperate Housewives*, they can employ individual tactics to negotiate and deal with the various difficulties they have to face, which enable empowerment and choice.[4] For example, when Longoria finds herself dissatisfied with being used as a trophy wife for her demanding husband, Carlos, but still requires his financial support, she begins an affair with the couple's teenage gardener. She thus fulfils her need for physical satisfaction without sacrificing her lifestyle. The trophy wife who is valued only for her physical desirability turns the tables and takes a male trophy lover who she values only for his physical desirability. The choices the women make may not always be agreeable but they do allow them a degree of empowerment in their life. This empowerment is limited, however, since it can only be achieved through the subversion of the patriarchal society in which the women live. The desperate housewives do not experience equality, they experience inequality and injustice in their always heterosexual, domestic relationships. But they use individual tactics of guile and inventiveness to counter the patriarchal structure around them.

Interestingly, although the series is marketed as one involving a collective of female friends, the women rarely, if ever, work together to resolve any issues they may encounter. In line with the postfeminist ideology that promotes the empowerment of the individual woman over the collective group, the women employ individual tactics to deal with their domestic issues.

The second example of the use of Eve imagery in *Desperate Housewives* promotional material is the promotional trailer for the second season of the show, which ran during the break of NFL's Opening Kickoff in 2005. The trailer included each of the women in short scenes involving red apples.[5] The theme of the trailer is the word 'juicy': the advertisement is set to the song *Juicy* by the band Ezra,[6] and each woman, at the end of

---

4.   Debbie Rodan, '*Desperate Housewives*: The Popularising of a Western Global Feminism', *Illumina* 1 (2006/7), pp. 1-10.

5.   The *Desperate Housewives* Season Two trailer can be seen on the internet at: http://www.youtube.com/watch?v=vYCg7k8DJEE (accessed 7 November 2012).

6.   Ezra, *Juicy* (Artermis, 2005).

her scene, mouths 'juicy' to the camera. 'Juicy' can be used to describe many things—the bright red apples that form the major theme of the advertisement, the plots involving the characters that are alluded to during the trailer and the women themselves, who act seductively and slightly menacingly throughout the scenes. The trailer begins with Teri Hatcher (Susan), in a black silk dress, walking seductively towards the camera while the blue sky rains red apples. The scene cuts to a close-up of a clock, which winds quickly forward, and then Hatcher, still walking seductively, enters a kitchen, where she opens a silver refrigerator only to be knocked to the ground by hundreds of red apples falling out. There is a close-up of Hatcher's amused expression as the viewer sees that she has landed next to a male arm. When the camera pans out, the viewer can see that the male arm belongs to her on/off love-interest in the show, Mike, who bends in to kiss her. Hatcher returns the kiss, winks at the camera and mouths the word 'juicy' before throwing a red apple into a bowl.

The camera then cuts to a different scene, where Marcia Cross (Bree), also wearing a black silk dress, is in her kitchen, preparing to slice a red apple. As she cuts the apple open, blood pours from its core (the blood is the same shade as the apple). The viewer then sees Cross holding the knife by her side as it drips blood. She looks at the camera, smiling seductively and mouths the word 'juicy'. A droplet of blood hits water and the trailer is cut to Felicity Huffman (Lynette), who is wearing a black business suit and juggling red apples. Her husband enters the scene, holding one of their small children, and throws her a black brief-case. She catches the case and grins ruefully at the camera and mouths 'juicy'. The scene now changes to Eva Longoria (Gabriella), who lies in a bath of red apples. She is wearing nothing but an expression of sensual pleasure. Longoria looks to the window and sees that her husband, Carlos, is watching her through the glass. She gasps before the scene changes briefly to an image of Carlos locked in a prison cell. Again, the scene cuts back to Longoria—now wearing a black silk dress—who throws an apple up and down in her hand. She looks into the camera with a satisfied wink and mouths 'juicy'.

The final scene of the trailer is based in the garden of Eden. Edie (Nicolette Sheridan), wearing the obligatory black silk dress, preens herself in front of an ornate mirror that is attached to the trunk of the tree of the knowledge of good and evil. While she is grooming her hair she is surprised by the appearance of a snake, which drops down in front of her face and drops a red apple into her hand. The scene cuts to the words, 'Tempting isn't it?', and then back to a close up of Sheridan's mouth as she repeats the word 'juicy' once more to the camera. The trailer then gives the time and date of the opening show of the new season.

Figure 4.5. *Eva Longoria in* Desperate Housewives *promotional TV trailer,* *ABC Network, August 2005*

After the enormous success of its opening season, ABC created this highly sophisticated trailer to promote the second series of *Desperate Housewives*. Making the most of the now hugely famous actresses, who have become valuable commodities in their own right, the trailer creates a *Femme Fatale* theme around each of the women. The forthcoming plots that the characters will be involved in during the second season are presented in terms of mildly menacing surreal scenes. The overwhelming presence of red apples represents the individual choices the women will make and the deceptions they will undertake as a consequence of these choices. For instance, Susan is overwhelmed with romantic choices and deceptions in the next series, which is signified by the apples raining down around her and the scene where she is knocked to the floor by apples cascading from her refrigerator. Bree's scene links the red apple with blood and death because the forthcoming plot centring on her character will involve her being implicated in the death of her husband. Lynette will deal with juggling motherhood, career and marriage in the second season, so her scene in the trailer depicts her juggling red apples in the same way that she will juggle the choices and deceptions in her life. Gabriella, arguably the most openly deceptive of all the *Desperate Housewives* characters, is filmed bathing sensually in the red apples. She will enjoy her choices and deceptions in the second series, which centre around the imprisonment of her husband, Carlos. Edie, who will be

offered choices and temptation during the second season of the show, has
an apple dropped in her hand by a serpent from the tree of knowledge of
good and evil.

While the function of the apples in the trailer undoubtedly points to
the basic theme of choice and deception in the show and the complex
plots of the next season, apples further function as a representation of the
desirability of the female stars. The female celebrities are tempting the
viewer to watch the second season of the show with their sexuality,
which is played upon by the choice of black silk evening dresses as outfits
for the women and also the undercurrent of sexual suggestion that carries
through the trailer. For instance, the repetition of the word 'juicy'
describes not only the dramatic forthcoming plot-lines but also the
women themselves, who are being described in the same terms as the
forbidden fruit.

Figure 4.6. Desperate Housewives, Forbidden Fruit *website*, 2006

Advertising for the *Desperate Housewives: Forbidden Fruit* fragrance,
which was released at the same as the second-season promotional trailer,
builds on the themes emphasized in the short promotional film. In the
print advertisement for the perfume, the female stars of the show all wear
the same outfits as in the trailer and, again echoing the scenes from the
trailer; they are all connected with the red apple 'forbidden fruit'. The
five main stars of the popular ABC comedy-drama series are pictured in a
circular shot, lying on a bed of red apples.

For example, in the 2005 perfume advertisement for the *Desperate Housewives* fragrance, *Forbidden Fruit*, advertisers again exploit the combination of Eve and the ultimate achievement of power through female sexuality—the female celebrity—to sell products to female consumers. Figure 4.1 shows the website for the *Forbidden Fruit* perfume, where it is described as 'the new seductive fragrance'. The Adam and Eve image from the *Desperate Housewives* opening credits decorates the box and the show's five female stars, immersed in a sea of forbidden fruit, are positioned around the central display of the product. Riser Media, the creative design agency hired by ABC to create the promotional site for the perfume, commented that it 'made beautiful women instinctively flock like the salmon of Capistrano'.[7]

Now, as famous celebrities, who are known by their own names more than those of their characters, the desperate housewives have become a highly lucrative sales vehicle for the show's merchandise. Used as a promotional image to sell perfume to the many fans of the show, the apple, in combination with the female celebrity holding it, offers the spectator-buyer the opportunity to become part of the *Desperate Housewives*. Just as the Adam and Eve scene in the opening credits and the end of that scene, when each of the characters is pictured holding an apple from the tree, signify the problematic power dynamics of male/female domestic relationships and the various 'sins' of each of the *Desperate Housewives* female characters (e.g. infidelity, preferring career to childcare, arson and taking non-prescription drugs to cope with the stress of motherhood, to name but a few), the image of the celebrities seductively holding an apple in the print advertisement for the *Desperate Housewives* perfume connotes the desirability and empowerment of those women and tempts consumers with the offer of somehow buying those same qualities through the perfume.

The show *Desperate Housewives* has always been concerned with the difficulties of domesticity for contemporary women (how to stem the resentment of having to put a successful career on hold when one has four children to look after and child-care is still seen as primarily the mother's responsibility; how to deal with the heart-break and humiliation of a husband's infidelity; how to negotiate one's own infidelity etc.) and it resonated with the feelings and experiences of millions of female viewers. The empowerment of the *Desperate Housewives* characters, however, involved each of them working within the patriarchal structure

7. See http://www.risermedia.com/website/forbidden-fruit/ (accessed 7 November 2012).

of society, individually subverting and undermining its limiting effects on them. The show translates this individual subversion of the traditional familial structures of patriarchy into postfeminist empowerment, as the women use their sexuality, desirability, guile and inventiveness to negotiate their way around the difficulties caused by their relationships with men.

The depiction of the postfeminist empowerment of the *Desperate Housewives* female characters in the opening credits of the show, and the representation of the actresses as Eves in postfeminist advertising, is no more than a way of marketing a form of limited female empowerment within a patriarchal structure. Far from returning to female power after the achievement of equality, women who subscribe to postfeminist ideology that promotes the empowerment of the individual by whatever means she needs to employ are actually using the same skills and wiles attributed to 'cunning' or 'devious' women who have attempted to subvert patriarchy throughout the ages. Postfeminism, in this package, is nothing new; in fact it is even older than the images it recycles.

BIBLIOGRAPHY

Abrams, D., *et al.*, 'Evaluating Stranger and Acquaintance Rape: The Role of Benevolent Sexism in Perpetrator Blame and Recommended Sentence Length', *Law & Human Behavior* 3.28 (2004), pp. 295-303.

—'Perceptions of Stranger and Acquaintance Rape: The Role of Benevolent and Hostile Sexism in Victim Blame and Rape Proclivity', *Journal of Personality & Social Psychology* 1.84 (2003), pp. 111-25.

Adams, Carol J., *The Pornography of Meat* (London: Continuum, 2003).

Allen, Stuart Lee, *In the Devil's Garden: The Sinful History of Forbidden Food* (Toronto: Canongate, 2002).

Allen, Virginia M., *The Femme Fatale: Erotic Icon* (Troy, NY: Whitston Publishing, 1983).

Allende, Isabel, *Aphrodite: The Love of Food and the Food of Love* (London: Flamingo, 1999).

Asher, Rebecca, *Shattered: Modern Motherhood and the Illusion of Equality* (New York: Harvill Secker, 2011).

Babington, Bruce, and Peter William Evans, *Biblical Epics: Sacred Narrative in the Hollywood Cinema* (Manchester: Manchester University Press, 1993).

—*Women, Seduction and Betrayal in Biblical Narrative* (Cambridge: Cambridge University Press, 1997).

—'With a Song in her Heart: Listening to Scholars Listening for Miriam', in Athalya Brenner (ed.), *A Feminist Companion to Exodus to Deuteronomy* (Sheffield: Sheffield Academic Press, 1994), pp. 243-54.

—'Eating their Words', in Brenner and van Henten (eds.), *Food and Drink*, pp. 215-22.

Bade, Patrick, *Femme Fatale: Images of Evil and Fascinating Women* (New York: Mayflower Books, 1979).

—*Lethal Love: Feminist Literary Readings of Biblical Love Stories* (Bloomington: Indiana University Press, 1987).

Baumgardner, Jennifer, and Amy Richards, *ManifestA: Feminism, the Future and Young Women* (New York: Farrar, Straus & Giroux, 2000).

BBC Radio 4, 'The Impact of Borrowing and Debt on Women's Lives', *Woman's Hour* (14 June 2005).

Benedict, Helen, *Virgin or Vamp: How the Press Covers Sex Crimes* (Oxford: Oxford University Press, 1992).

Benedix, Beth Hawkins (ed.), *Subverting Scriptures: Critical Reflections on the Use of the Bible* (New York: Palgrave Macmillan, 2009).

Berger, John, *Ways of Seeing* (London: Penguin Books, 1977).

Bird, Phyllis A., *Missing Persons and Mistaken Identities: Women and Gender in Ancient Israel* (Minneapolis: Fortress Press, 1997).

Bohner, G., and N. Schwarz, 'The Threat of Rape: Its Psychological Impact on Non-victimized Women', in D.M. Buss and N. Malamuth (eds.), *Sex, Power, Conflict: Evolutionary and Feminist Perspectives* (Oxford: Oxford University Press, 1996), pp. 162-75.

Brenner, Athalya (ed.), *A Feminist Companion to Genesis* (Sheffield: Sheffield Academic Press, 1993).

Brenner, Athalya, and Jan Willem van Henten (eds.), *Food and Drink in the Biblical Worlds* (Atlanta, GA: Society of Biblical Literature, 1999).

Brooks, Ann, *Postfeminisms: Feminism, Cultural Theory, and Cultural Forms* (London: Routledge, 1997).

Brown, Francis, S.R. Driver and Charles A. Briggs, *A Hebrew and English Lexicon of the Old Testament* (Oxford: Clarendon Press, 1907).

Buchwald, Emilie, Pamela R. Fletcher and Martha Roth (eds.), *Transforming a Rape Culture* (Minneapolis: Milkweed Editions, 1993).

Campbell, Delilah, 'This Article Degrades Advertisements', *Trouble and Strife* 35 (1997), pp. 30-39.

Ciriello, Sarah, 'Commodification of Women: Morning, Noon and Night', in Buchwald and Roth (eds.), *Transforming a Rape Culture*, pp. 265-81.

Clines, David J.A., *What Does Eve Do to Help? And Other Readerly Questions to the Old Testament* (Sheffield: JSOT Press, 1990).

Clines, David J.A. (ed.), *Dictionary of Classical Hebrew* (8 vols.; Sheffield: Sheffield Phoenix Press, 1993–2011).

Coppock, Vicki, Deena Haydon and Ingrid Richter, *The Illusions of Post-Feminism: New Women, Old Myths* (London: Taylor & Francis, 1995).

Corré, Joseph, and Serena Rees, *Agent Provocateur: A Celebration of Femininity* (London: Carlton Books, 1999).

Cortese, Anthony J., *Provocateur: Images of Women and Minorities in Advertising* (Lanham: Rowman & Littlefield, 1999).

Coward, R., *Female Desire* (London: Paladin, 1984).

Crittendon, Anne, *The Price of Motherhood: Why the Most Important Job in the World Is Still the Least Valued* (New York: Owl Books, 2002).

Culbertson, Philip, and Elaine M. Wainwright (eds.), *The Bible in/and Popular Culture: A Creative Encounter* (Atlanta: Society of Biblical Literature, 2010).

Curran, J., *et al.* (eds.), *Bending Reality: The State of the Media* (London: Pluto Press, 1986).

Dally, Ann, *Inventing Motherhood: The Consequences of an Ideal* (New York: Schocken Books, 1982).

Danna, Sammy R., 'Sexier and More Sensitive: The Changing Advertising Image of Males in the 1990s', in Luigi Manca and Alessandra Manca, *Gender and Utopia in Advertising: A Critical Reader* (Lisle, IL: Propcopian Press, 1994), pp. 73-86.

De Graf, John *et al.*, *Affluenza: The All Consuming Epidemic* (San Francisco: Berret-Koehler Publishers, 2005).

DEMOS, 'Generation Broke: The Growth of Debt among Young Americans', US Government Briefing Paper (2005).

Douglas, Susan J., and Meredith W. Michaels, *The Mommy Myth: The Idealizaton of Motherhood and How it Has Undermined Women* (New York: Free Press, 2004).

Draut, Tamara, *Strapped: Why America's 20 and 30 Somethings Can't Get Ahead* (New York: Anchor Books, 2005).

Dyer, Richard, *Advertising as Communication* (London: Methuen, 1982).

Exum, J. Cheryl, *Plotted, Shot and Painted: Cultural Representations of Biblical Women* (Sheffield: Sheffield Academic Press, 1996).

Exum, J. Cheryl, and Ela Nutu (eds.), *Between the Text and the Canvas* (Sheffield: Sheffield Phoenix Press, 2007).

Fewell, Danna Nolan, and David M. Gunn, *Gender, Power and Promise: The Subject of the Bible's First Story* (Nashville: Abingdon Press, 1993).

Forbes 100 (2006), http://www.forbes.com/2006/06/12/06celebrities_money-power-celebrities-list_land.html.

Friend, Tab, 'The Rise of "Do Me" Feminism', *Esquire* (February 1994), pp. 48-56.

Gill, Rosalind, *Gender and the Media* (Cambridge, MA: Polity Press, 2007).

Gillis, Stacy, and Rebecca Munford, *Feminism and Popular Culture: Explorations in Postfeminism* (London: I.B. Tauris, 2007).

Goffman, Erving, *Gender Advertisements* (London: Macmillan, 1979).

Goldman, Robert, *Reading Ads Socially* (London: Routledge, 1992).

Goldman, Robert, Deborah Heath and Sharon L. Smith, 'Commodity Feminism', *Critical Studies in Mass Communication* 8 (1991), pp. 333-51.

Gurley Brown, Helen, *Sex and the Single Girl: The Unmarried Woman's Guide to Men* (New York: Open Road Iconic Books, 2012).

Hall, Stuart, 'Media Power and Class Power', in Curran *et al.* (eds.), *Bending Reality*, pp. 5-14.

Hanson, Helen, and Catherine O'Rawe (eds.), *The Femme Fatale: Images, Histories, Contexts* (Hampshire: Palgrave Macmillan, 2010).

Harris, Anita M., *Future Girl: Young Women in the Twenty-First Century* (London: Routledge, 2004).

Hatton, Erin, and Mary Nell Trautner, 'Images of Powerful Women in the Age of "Choice Feminism"', *Journal of Gender Studies* 22.2 (forthcoming 2013).

Hedgecock, Jennifer, *The Femme Fatale in Victorian Literature: The Danger and the Sexual Threat* (New York: Cambria Press, 2008).

Heywood, Leslie, and Jennifer Drake, 'Introduction', in Heywood and Drake (eds.), *Third Wave Agenda: Being Feminist, Doing Feminism* (Minneapolis: University of Minnesota Press, 2003), pp. 1-24.

Holland, J., C. Ramazanoglu and S. Scott, 'AIDS: From Panic Stations to Relations', *Sociology* 24.3 (1990), pp. 499-518.

Holland, Janet *et al.*, 'Sex, Gender and Power: Young Women's Sexuality in the Shadow of AIDS', *Sociology of Health and Illness* 12.3 (1990), pp. 336-50.

Hopkins, Martha, and Randall Lockridge, *New Intercourses: An Aphrodisiac Cookbook* (London: Terrace Publishing, 2007).

Hurley, Liz, *Having it All: Love, Success, Sex, Money Even if You're Starting with Nothing* (New York: Simon & Schuster, 1982).

James, Oliver, *Affluenza* (London: Vermilion, 2007).

Jobling, David, *The Sense of Biblical Narrative. II. Structural Analyses in the Hebrew Bible* (Sheffield: JSOT Press, 1986).

Johnson, K.K.P., 'Attributions about Date Rape: Impact of Clothing, Sex, Money Spent, Date Type, and Perceived Similarity', *Family and Consumer Sciences Research Journal* 23 (1995), pp. 292-311.

Kamenetez, Anya, *Generation Debt: Why Now Is a Terrible Time to Be Young* (New York: Riverhead Books, 2006).

Kestner, Joseph A., *Mythology and Misogyny: The Social Discourse of Nineteenth-Century British Classical-Subject Painting* (Madison: University of Wisconsin Press, 1989).

Kidd Stewart, Janet, 'Generation IOU: Credit Card Debt and College Loans Are Creating Financial Hardship for Many of Today's Young Working Women', *The Chicago Tribune* (27 April 2005).

Kilbourne, Jean, *Deadly Persuasion: Why Women and Girls Must Fight the Addictive Power of Advertising* (New York: Free Press, 1999).

Kim, L.S., '"Sex and the Single Girl" in Postfeminism', *Television and New Media* 2.4 (2001), pp. 319-34.

Kimmelman, Reuven, 'The Seduction of Eve and the Exegetical Politics of Gender', *Biblical Interpretation* 4 (1996), pp. 1-39.

Landy, Francis, *Paradoxes of Paradise: Identity and Difference in the Song of Songs* (Sheffield: Almond Press, 1983).

Lanser, Susan S., '(Feminist) Criticism in the Garden: Inferring Genesis 2–3', in Hugh C. White (ed.), *Speech Act Theory and Biblical Criticism* (Semeia, 41; Atlanta: Scholars Press, 1987), pp. 67-84.

Lees, S., *Losing Out: Sexuality and Adolescent Girls* (London: Hutchinson, 1986).

Levy, Ariel, *Female Chauvinist Pigs: Women and the Rise of Raunch Culture* (New York: Free Press, 2005).

Lotz, Amanda D., 'Postfeminist Television Criticism: Rehbilitating Critical Terms and Identifying Postfeminist Attributes', *Feminist Media Studies* 1.1 (2001), pp. 105-21.

Mabry, A. Rochelle, 'About a Girl: Female Subjectivity and Sexuality in Contemporary "Chick" Lit Culture', in Suzanne Ferris and Malory Young (eds.), *Chick Lit: The New Woman's Fiction* (London: Routledge, 2005), pp. 191-207.

Mackinnon, Kenneth, *Uneasy Pleasures: The Male as Erotic Object* (London: Cygnus Arts, 1997).

Mann, Patricia S., *Micro-Politics: Agency in a Postfeminist Era* (Minneapolis: University of Minnesota Press, 1994).

Manning, Robert D., *Credit Card Nation: The Consequences of America's Addiction to Credit* (New York: Basic Books, 2002).

McG, *Charlie's Angels* (Sony Pictures Home Entertainment UK, 2000).

—*Charlie's Angels 2: Full Throttle* (Sony Pictures Home Entertainment UK, 2003).

Menon, Elizabeth K., *Evil by Design: The Creation and Marketing of the Femme Fatale* (Urbana: University of Illinois Press, 2006).

Meyers, Carol L., *Discovering Eve: Ancient Israelite Woman in Context* (Oxford: Oxford University Press, 1988).

Miles, Margaret R., *Carnal Knowing: Female Nakedness and Religious Meaning in the Christian West* (Kent: Burns & Oates, 1992).

Millum, Trevor, *Images of Woman: Advertising in Women's Magazines* (London: Chatto & Windus, 1975).

Milne P., 'The Patriarchal Stamp of Scripture: The Implications of Structuralist Analyses for Feminist Hermeneutics', in Brenner (ed.), *A Feminist Companion to Genesis*, pp. 146-72.

Moles Kaupp, Cristina, *The Erotic Cookbook* (London: Fusion Press, 2002).

Moseley, Rachel, and Jacinda Read, '"Having it *Ally*": Popular Television (Post-) Feminism', in *Feminist Media Studies* 2.2 (2002), pp. 231-49.

Negra, Diane, *What a Girl Wants? Fantasizing the Reclamation of Self in Postfeminism* (London: Routledge, 2009).

Negra, Diane, and Yvonne Tasker, *Interrogating Postfeminism: Gender and the Politics of Popular Culture* (London: Duke University Press, 2007).

—'In Focus: Postfeminism and Contemporary Media Studies', *Cinema Journal* 44.2 (2005), pp. 107-10.

Norris, Pamela, *The Story of Eve* (London: Papermac, 1999).

O'Kane, Martin, *Painting the Text: The Artist as Biblical Interpreter* (Sheffield: Sheffield Phoenix Press, 2007).

Pardes, Ilana, *Countertraditions in the Bible: A Feminist Approach* (Cambridge, MA: Harvard University Press, 1993).

Perle, Liz, *Money, a Memoir: Women, Emotions and Cash* (New York: Henry Holt & Co., 2006).

Projansky, Sarah, *Watching Rape: Film and Television in Postfeminist Culture* (New York: New York University Press, 2001).

Pronger, Brian, *The Arena of Masculinity: Sports, Homosexuality and the Meaning of Sex* (London: Gay Men's Press, 1994).

Rad, Gerhard von, *Genesis: A Commentary* (Philadelphia: Westminster Press, 1972).

Ramis, Harry, *Bedazzled* (Twentieth Century Fox, 1999).

Reiley, Amy, *Fork Me, Spoon Me: The Sensual Cookbook* (London: Life of Reiley, 2010).

Rodan, Debbie, 'Desperate Housewives: The Popularising of a Western Global Postfeminism', *Illumina* 1 (2006/7), pp. 1-10.

Ross, Andrew, *No Respect: Intellectuals and Popular Culture* (London: Routledge, 1989).

Sanders, Theresa, *Approaching Eden: Adam and Eve in Popular Culture* (London: Rowman & Littlefield, 2009).

Schungel-Straumann, Helen, 'On the Creation of Man and Woman in Genesis 1–3: The History and Reception of the Texts Reconsidered', in Brenner (ed.), *A Feminist Companion to Genesis*, pp. 53-76.

Scurlock, James D., *Maxed Out: Hard Times, Easy Credit* (London: HarperCollins, 2007).

Sherwood, Yvonne, *A Biblical Text and its Afterlives: The Survival of Jonah in Western Culture* (Cambridge: Cambridge University Press, 2000).

Showalter, Elaine, *Sexual Anarchy: Gender and Culture at the Fin-de-siècle* (London: Bloomsbury, 1991).

Slatkin, Wendy, 'Maternity and Sexuality in the 1890s', *Women's Art Journal* 1.1 (1980), pp. 13-19.

Smith, Joan, *Hungry for You: From Cannibalism to Seduction—A Book of Food* (London: Vintage, 1997).

Stott, Rebecca, *The Fabrication of the Late-Victorian Femme Fatale: The Kiss of Death* (London: Macmillan Press, 1992).

Stratton, Jon, *The Desirable Body: Cultural Fetishism and the Erotics of Consumption* (Manchester: Manchester University Press, 1996).

Style, Christopher, and Scott S. Tobis, *The 'Desperate Housewives' Cookbook: Juicy Dishes and Saucy Bits* (New York: Hyperion, 2006).

Sullivan, Teresa A., *et al.*, *As We Forgive our Debtors: Bankruptcy and Consumer Credit in America* (Washington, DC: Beard Books, 1999).

Trible, Phyllis, *God and the Rhetoric of Sexuality* (London: SCM Press, 1992).

Veenker, Ronald A., 'Forbidden Fruit: Ancient Near Eastern Sexual Metaphors', *Hebrew Union College Annual* 70–71 (1999–2000), pp. 57-73.

Viki, G. Tendayi, and Dominic Abrams, 'But She Was Unfaithful: Benevolent Sexism and Reactions to Rape Victims Who Violate Traditional Gender Role Expectations—Brief Report', *Sex Roles: A Journal of Research* 47 (2002), pp. 289-93.

Wallis, Claudia, 'The Case for Staying at Home', *Time* (22 March 2004), pp. 50-59.

Walsh, Carey Ellen, *Exquisite Desire: Religion, the Erotic, and the Song of Songs* (Minneapolis: Fortress Press, 2000).

Warner, Judith, 'The Myth of the Perfect Mother: Why it Drives Real Women Crazy', *Newsweek* (21 February 2005), pp. 42-49.

Williamson, Judith, *Decoding Advertisements: Ideology and Meaning in Advertising* (London: Marion Boyers Publishers, 2000).

Wolf, Naomi, *The Beauty Myth: How Images of Beauty Are Used against Women* (London: Vintage, 1991).

Woolf, Virginia, *A Room of One's Own* (London: Flamingo, 1994).

INDEX OF AUTHORS

Lightning Source UK Ltd.
Milton Keynes UK
UKOC01n1218010814

236161UK00006BA/33/P

9 781907 534713